The Contemporary Presidency

The Contemporary Presidency

DOROTHY BUCKTON JAMES

PEGASUS   NEW YORK

The Contemporary Presidency is part of a series,
"Studies in Contemporary American Politics,"
published by Pegasus under the General Editor-
ship of Richard E. Morgan, Columbia University.

For Judson

ACKNOWLEDGMENTS

It is a pleasure to be able to express appreciation publicly for the assistance which I have received in writing this volume. While its errors are mine, its better aspects have been aided by many to whom I am deeply grateful:

Professors Lawrence Chamberlain and Richard Neustadt, who first introduced me to these questions when I was a graduate student at Columbia University.

Professors Roger Davidson of University of California at Santa Barbara, Richard Morgan of Columbia University, Gerald Pomper of Rutgers University, and Kenneth Smith of Hunter College, City University of New York, for their perceptive suggestions on the manuscript.

Professor Judson L. James of City College, City University of New York, my most cherished critic.

My students, a constant inspiration.

Introduction

Attitudes toward the use and expansion of Presidential power are related to broader aspects of an author's value system: whether his preferences for political organization are "conservative" or "liberal." The American context provides a unique definition for these differences. As Louis Hartz has suggested, the American political tradition is basically a liberal one. America was "born free" in the sense that it never experienced the static inequalities of a feudal system. Moreover, the period of its birth coincided with a period when the liberal principles of John Locke had been widely disseminated. They seemed so appropriate and self-evident in the American context that Locke's principles became "a massive national cliche."[1] Therefore, conservatism was "twisted entirely out of shape by the liberal flow of American history."[2] In consequence, as Gunnar Myrdal has suggested: "America is . . . conservative. . . . But the principles conserved are liberal and some, indeed, are radical."[3] The distinction between conservatism and liberalism in the European context indicates the greatly altered meaning of these terms in American usage, which in turn throws light upon contemporary American attitudes toward expansion of Presidential power.

The European conservative tradition was expressed in works by Edmund Burke, Joseph de Maistre, Louis de Bonald, and Johann Fichte. Its unifying themes were a pessimism about human nature (heavy stress on "original sin"), an emphasis on hierarchy (heavy stress on human inequalities), tradition and religion (the existing constitution of a society ought to be the object of a reverence akin to religion). Above all, it viewed the individual as receiving his significance and rights from his membership in the community.

The American conservative rejects most of these premises. He emphasizes individual rights against state power, is more optimistic about the nature of man (though not so optimistic as his liberal compatriot), and is unwilling to accord existing constitutional arrangements much reverence. Rather, he would prefer to repeal constitutional developments, at least those since Franklin Roosevelt. He is, in short, in the ironic position of conserving liberal values.[4]

Liberalism in the European context began in a protest against authoritarianism. Therefore, its negative aspects were foremost for centuries.[5] Its purpose was to liberate the individual from religious, political, economic, and social coercion. Its central tenet held that the free individual was the proper goal of social policy. Individuals were empowered to seek private ends that would presumably be limited by a rational propensity toward decent behavior. In its concern for freeing the individual, liberal thought underwent three major periods of development. Initially, the work of John Locke focused on freedom from authoritarianism by taking its stand on an assumed natural law which postulated a right to life, liberty, and estate for everyone. In Locke's theory, government was formed by a contract of free individuals who established it for the sole purpose of executing the natural law. If government failed in this function, the individuals would be free to form another contract.

Following David Hume, later liberal theorists demolished the concept of a social contract based on natural law, substituting a utilitarian justification for government: that government was considered best which provided the greatest happiness for the greatest number. This was the basis for Adam Smith's demand that governments avoid interference in the economic order. Smith assumed that there was a natural harmony in the economic order (expressed by the image of an "invisible hand") which would work toward the greatest good of the greatest number if unrestrained. That government was considered best, therefore, which governed least.

The third phase of liberal thought stressed an organic relationship between the individual and his society. In the transition of liberal thought from utilitarianism to organic liberalism, John Stuart Mill emphasized the concept that the foundation of liberty was not a mere formula of law nor restrictions upon the government, but the idea of individual development which depended upon the manner in which society was organized. At the end of the nineteenth century T. H. Green postulated the tenets of organic liberalism: liberty must not be merely negative (*freedom from* external coercion); it must be positive (*freedom for* personal development). While government could not make people moral by law, it could remove hindrances to their moral development. Politics could be a means for creating social conditions that made moral development possible.

Organic liberalism was the philosophical foundation of the modern "service state." Because individual growth and development might be inhibited by ignorance, hunger, disease, or poverty, the state tried to eliminate these conditions through a variety of measures such as compulsory education, compulsory health regulations and safety standards, unemployment insurance, social security, aid to dependent children, medicare, and public health clinics.

The Locke/Smith versions of liberal thought form the core of thought that is termed "conservative" in America. An American conservative stresses individual freedom from political, religious, or economic coercion, and protection of life, liberty, and property as the sole valid governmental function. As a means to safeguard individual rights he desires that all exercise of governmental power be checked and balanced, and that government be limited in size and scope. He, therefore, evidences particular hostility to any growth of power in the national government, especially in a single individual such as the Executive. This antagonism toward the contemporary development of the Presidency was expressed by Edward S. Corwin.[6] He considered only the Constitution and long customary usage to be the accepted sources of Presidential power. Therefore, he held that the President must be limited to five roles: Chief of State, Chief Diplomat, Commander-in-Chief, Chief Legislator, and Chief Administrator. Any additional functions were viewed as dangerous "personalization" of the office that he desired to restrict and contain. In evaluating recent Presidents, Corwin considered Franklin Roosevelt to have been most dangerous because of his "personalization," whereas President Eisenhower's failure to innovate received the author's highest praise.

Twentieth-century American liberals are proponents of organic liberalism. They consider the modern service state to be necessary to provide individuals with positive freedom, and therefore tend to approve of the contemporary development of Presidential power. Indeed, many believe that the President remains too restricted within the American system of checks and balances. Such concern for the limitations on Presidential power was expressed by Richard Neustadt.[7] He believed that the President's ability to initiate could not depend on constitutionally defined roles that merely indicated services which the President was obliged to perform without any assurance of success. Therefore, Corwin's analysis was considered irrelevant because roles do not necessarily bring power, but merely make the President a clerk, providing services for others. Neustadt believed power to stem from the personality of the man in office: "Presidential power is the power to persuade." This persuasion rested upon three factors: the President's professional reputation, his public prestige, and the bargaining position of the office. The most dangerous man for the office would not be one who personalized it, but rather a political amateur lacking the skill and insight to use these tools to their greatest advantage. Of recent Presidents, Franklin Roosevelt received the highest praise while Dwight Eisenhower was considered most dangerous.

An analysis of the Presidency which blended aspects of conservative thought with a predominantly liberal outlook was written by Clinton Rossiter.[8] In addition to the five constitutional roles accepted by Edward Corwin, Rossiter added five that Corwin would have viewed as personalization: Chief of Party, Voice of the People, World Leader, Protector of the Peace, and Manager of Prosperity. His evaluation of recent Presidents was similar to that of Richard Neustadt, but he showed great concern for the *need* for limitations upon the exercise of Presidential power.

The present volume accepts the need for an active, innovative government, considers that the Presidency must be the major source of policy initiation within the contemporary American political context, and agrees that Presidential power is heavily dependent on the perception and persuasive skill of the individual in office. However, there seem to be weaknesses in liberal analysis of the Presidency which need correction.

Presidential power is defined in terms of a capacity for successful innovation, but the innovations that are proposed rarely originate with the President. Rather, he chooses among the proposals that his advisers present to him. Furthermore, successful innovation depends on the spirit and means with which the policies are administered. Liberal emphasis on increasing Presidential power tends to obscure the fact that the consequence of increased power for any President is increased power in the hands of a bureaucracy over which he can exercise only marginal control.

There is also an assumption in this writing that the President will be liberal. He should be powerful because it is assumed that he will work for the interest of the country. The deep frustration that liberals have felt with President Johnson's Vietnamese War policy has exposed the flaw in that assumption. As one writer has suggested:

> . . . Now they find themselves in the awkward position of not liking what President Johnson has done with Presidential power in Vietnam, and yet not knowing quite how to limit his power in order to change the policies they oppose. . . . The liberals are now trying to restrain the very powers they wanted in the past, and don't know how to do it.[9]

A further aspect of Presidential power which has not been adequately considered is the fact that the contemporary President functions within two distinct policy areas: the sphere of domestic policy and the sphere of foreign and defense policy. It is the very distinction between these two spheres which forms the primary characteristic of the contemporary Presidency. In domestic affairs the President's power is seriously limited through his dependence on the legislature and the bureaucracy, and by the fact that the public often views other political actors as equally legitimate spokesmen. The public is capable of assessing the relevance of domestic policies to its private concerns and will often reward pressure groups, the press, the opposition party, or other political actors for challenging the President's proposals. Therefore, great skill is needed by the

President to persuade these various elements to accept his proposals. Nevertheless, Richard Neustadt's analysis appears to be overstated in regard to the degree of limitations and restrictions that must be overcome. In opposing Corwin's emphasis on traditional roles, Neustadt has underplayed their significance. While he considered professional reputation, public prestige, and the bargaining position of the office to be the basis for persuasion, his writing was devoted primarily to the first two sources. Yet the bargaining position of the office includes its "clerkship," for as Neustadt wrote, the President's services are in demand throughout Washington. He has a relationship of mutual dependence with the legislative branch and enjoys unequalled opportunities to gain a public hearing for his proposals. Although there are many limitations on the exercise of his power in the domestic sphere, he does have tools and assets that should be considered more fully.

Whereas the President is beset by irksome restrictions in initiating domestic policy which necessitate a continuous process of bargaining and compromise with the legislature, in foreign relations and especially defense he has extraordinary leeway. As will be detailed in Chapter IV, public opinion in these areas is weak and unstructured but accords the President preeminence over any other spokesman. His traditional roles of Commander-in-Chief and Chief of State place him in a position that seriously handicaps any opponent. Limitations exist, but not from his constitutional rival, Congress. It is the thesis of this volume that the contemporary American Presidency is an institution characterized by paradox and imbalance, and that beyond skill in political manipulation, an individual's capacity to function in the office will be determined by his personal sense of grace and style.

Chapter I indicates some of the assets and liabilities of the process of attaining office and suggests the primary characteristics of the American political system which form the context within which the President must operate. This is followed in Chapter II by an analysis of the twentieth-century changes that have irrevocably altered the Presidential role. Chapters III and IV consider the domestic and international contexts within which the President must function. The book concludes with an analysis of qualities essential to effective use of Presidential power.

For purposes of this analysis, Franklin Roosevelt is viewed as a transitional figure, while primary emphasis is placed on the period from Harry Truman to the present. Admittedly, this is a brief time span from which to generalize, but it is one in which changes have occurred in the domestic and international context and the nature of Presidential and Congressional power which have substantially altered the nature of Presidential office. Because the Presidency has changed rapidly and irrevocably within the last two decades, it seems most relevant to analyze the *contemporary* nature of Presidential power.

Contents

I. Becoming President

THE PROCESS through which an individual must go to become President has consequences for the type of man who will be selected. That process includes obtaining his party's nomination and campaigning for office. But party organization and behavior is determined by the decentralization of American politics and the character of American political response. Any aspirant for Presidential office must come to terms with these factors if he hopes to be nominated and elected.

Throughout the process of becoming President, many traits of character, political knowledgeability, and effectiveness are tested. While most are relevant to the demands made upon a President, there remain some relevant skills that are never tested. Success in the process of becoming President is not a guarantee of success in office, but failure in that process does indicate a lack of the political acumen necessary to be able to function amid the complexities of the American political system.

Decentralization

Thoreau might have been describing the American political process when he wrote:

> If a man does not keep pace with his companions, perhaps it is because he hears a different drummer. Let him step to the music which he hears, however measured or far away.

Certainly, the theme of American political life would seem to have been scored exclusively for percussive and wind instruments. This multitude of drummers is a product of decentralization of the American political system stemming from separation of the executive and legislature, and from federalism. These two factors have created a variety of centers of responsibility, thereby assuring that the President's constituency, political risks, and responsibilities will be different from those of any other political actor in the system. Other actors will follow different drummers, thereby seriously limiting his capacity to function. Yet the relationship between the President and American political parties is one of mutual dependence. While his office has been shaped by the nature of the party system, that system has also been affected by his office, which is its primary centralizing force. Although he lacks sufficient control to be conductor, amid the varied percussive effects of American political life, the President's base drum is uniquely audible.

Federalism has promoted decentralization by providing a set of offices (governors and state legislators) which are partially independent of the national level, yet can have a significant influence on domestic policy. These offices present alternative points of access for interest groups, many of which are too small in the whole population to have an impact on national policy, but which are found disproportionately in one or several states and may exercise influence there. Thus, federalism gives a large number of people a stake in maintaining a diffusion of governmental authority.

Separation of the executive and legislature has promoted uncoordinated politics by providing each body with its own constituency and source of strength. While the President and Vice-President are the only nationally elected officials in America, not all elements of the nation are equally significant to their election. They are chosen by a majority of votes in the Electoral College, in which each state receives votes on the basis of its total number of United States Senators plus members of the House of Representatives. Since the Jacksonian era, all the Electoral votes of a state have been cast for the candidate who received the largest popular vote on Election Day in that state. Therefore, Presidential aspirants must be particularly responsive to large, competitive states, for a bare 50.1 per cent of the popular vote in New York State is sufficient to capture the state's entire forty-three Electoral votes, whereas even 99.9 per cent of the popular vote in New Mexico can bring no more than four Electoral votes. In order to reach at least a bare majority of the voters in a large, competitive state, a candidate must be especially sensitive to urban, industrial areas with their particular concerns such as labor, civil rights, minority protection, transportation, and welfare. Thus, the state winner-take-all feature of the Electoral College makes the effective constituency of any Presidential candidate an industrial, urban one. Few candidates other than Barry Goldwater have believed that one could reach the Presidency by carrying only the South, the mountains, and the desert. His overwhelming defeat in 1964 might seem to preclude further experimentation with the theory.

The primary differences in constituency between the Senate and President are now size and diversity, although from the First World War to the end of the Second, there was a third difference: a constitutional bias in favor of rural districts in the composition of the Senate because each state received equal representation and there were more states with primarily rural rather than industrial economies. However, urbanization accelerated so greatly after the Second World War that most states now have a sufficient number of organized voters in their urban centers to cause Senators to be attentive to their needs.

The rural bias of the House of Representatives has been more difficult to alter. Each state is allotted a number of Representatives on the basis of the state's population, but the size and shape of Congressional districts within the state are determined by state legislatures. Frequently, they have created gerrymandered Congressional districts with a rural bias. Even where conscious gerrymandering did not occur, the general reluctance of state legislatures to redraw district lines led to the serious underrepresentation of areas whose population was rapidly increasing, *i.e.*, suburban areas. Malapportionment has been estimated as giving rural interests a minimum of fifteen seats which should have gone to suburban or urban areas.[1] While that might be considered a small number in a House with 435 members, its true significance can better be judged by the fact that approximately fifteen votes has been the margin by which many major pieces of legislation have been passed or killed in the House since the 1930's. Changes are occurring slowly under the impact of the Supreme Court's redistricting decisions in the 1960's, but there continues to be a great deal of resistance to change.

Separation of the executive and legislative bodies also involves differences in electoral risk. Nationally, there is a highly competitive two-party system in which the minority party rarely polls below forty-five per cent of the popular vote. Because contests are usually so close, a Presidential candidate must attract marginal voters, *i.e.*, the "independent" voter and less committed members of the opposition party. This means that he must moderate his partisan stand.

Senators and Representatives less frequently encounter such limitations due to the relative rarity of competitive districts. Only one-fourth of the seats in Congressional districts are won by less than fifty-five per cent of the popular vote.[2] The office of Congressman can be a lifetime occupation in a one-party district, and often is. Therefore, despite the fortunes of the national party leader, many Representatives and Senators will be returned to office because they represent the majority party in a one-party district. Moreover, they will not even have faced competition in the nomination process if they are chosen in one of the large number of direct primaries in which there is no competition.[3] Thus, regardless of the wishes of national party leaders, especially the President, they are free to accumulate seniority, which is the major path to leadership and power in both houses.[4]

The decentralizing effect both of separation of executive and legislative bodies and of federalism are reinforced by the characteristics of competition within the parties. Candidates for either party's nomination for the national legislature are not chosen by national party leaders, but by direct primaries in their districts or by conventions organized by state party leaders. Voting data indicate that, with the exception of some one-party areas, voter turnout is generally low in party primaries and is not representative of the general electorate.[5] Therefore, control over Congressional careers is not at the party's national center, but among active local minorities and interest groups that can finance campaigns in the low-turnout party primaries. In any district or state where one party is dominant, that party's primary is the crucial point at which its representative is chosen. Election merely ratifies the choice made on Primary Day.

The character of American political response is one of the

major determinants of party organization and behavior. Major studies of levels of political information and ideology, partisan identification, and interest have shown a low level of interest and knowledge about party politics and public events in America. The leading study on American voting found that only about fifteen per cent of the electorate even come near voting on the basis of a well-considered, consistent ideology. At the opposite end of the spectrum, an even larger percentage (seventeen per cent) cast their ballots on the basis of no issue content whatsoever. Almost a majority of American voters (forty-five per cent) choose a Presidential candidate on the basis of benefits that groups to which they belong had received or were likely to receive from his administration. The remaining twenty-three per cent of the electorate were found to vote according to the nature of the times: if good they retained the party in power, if bad they threw the "rascals" out.[6]

Due to this low level of interest and attention to party politics and public events, the electorate is more aware of the words and actions of a party in power than of the opposition. The electorate judges retrospectively. Its principal role is that of appraiser of past events, performances, and actions.[7] Therefore, the opposition party profits more by the errors of the party in power than by the alternatives which it can offer. It gains votes most notably from among those groups who feel disappointed, disapproved of, or injured by the administration. For example, the primary strength of the Republican party in unseating Democrats from the Presidency in 1952 and 1968 was not provided by the novelty or appeal of its programs, but by the growing unrest caused by the Korean War and fear of corruption and Communist infiltration of government in 1952 and by the Vietnamese War and fear of civil disorder and violence in 1968.

When the decentralizing effects of federalism and separation of powers are reinforced by the direct primary system and a low level of political interest and knowledge among the electorate, it is clear that the political context within which the President must function presents a serious obstacle to fulfilling his role as leader of his party. His campaign for election and his policy proposals must of necessity reflect the decentralized, heterogeneous, non-ideological nature of his nation. Separate terms and constituencies make it possible for the President to be leader of a party that has only a minority of seats in the legislature. He will therefore have to entrust his legislative program to a leadership of the opposition party, as President Eisenhower had to do for six of his eight years in office and as President Nixon had to do on entering office. Even in the more usual circumstances in which the President is leader of the majority party in the legislature, that leadership does not assure that his party platform will be enacted. Legislators must represent the wishes of local party leaders and/or their constituents because these can exercise more direct control over political careers than can national party leaders who lack disciplinary authority. Therefore, legislators find it difficult to hold a party line in opposition to constituent wishes. This puts the President in the position of being titular leader of a party whose membership marches to many a "distant drummer."

Despite these handicaps to his capacity for leadership, the President has some influence on the party system because the Presidency and the party system are mutually interdependent. His significance for it lies in the fact that he is its major centralizing influence.[8] The office of President provides a reason for unification and cooperation among party factions because it is a single, indivisible office which can only be attained through a united effort. While American political parties take the form of loose coalitions, they necessarily center on the President. Because he and his Vice-President are the only nationally elected figures, he must create a broader coalition within the party than any other political actor. Once elected, this breadth enhances his access and tactical possibilities in internal party struggles. Moreover, partisan identification in America is almost totally a function of national political events, *i.e.*, voter images of the parties are formed on the basis of the party's actions and programs at the national level.[9] Major party realignments in bases of support and policy orientation have been responses to national events, especially those personalized by attachments to particular Presidents, such as the Civil War, or the Great Depression and New Deal.[10] As V. O. Key has written: "The governmental system may be federal but the voter in the polling booth usually is not."[11]

A further explanation for the growing influence of the President as a centralizing force within the American party system can be found in the fact that the public has come increasingly to expect him to be the major source of policy initiation in the political system, as will be discussed more fully in Chapters II and III. Institutional developments and the President's unique opportunities to gain publicity for his proposals and to associate them with his party provide special advantages for this. Furthermore, the formal apparatus and legitimacy he receives as titular leader of his party can be used advantageously. His success in coordinating the diverse elements of his party is not guaranteed, however. It depends upon his own skill and opportunities.

Beyond its centralizing influence, the office of President shapes the party system by its instrumental role in the maintenance of a two-party system. The fact that the candidate who receives the most popular votes in a state will receive that state's entire Electoral vote discourages the development of minor parties contesting for the Presidential office, since only established parties are likely to have the organization and following to be able to compete for it effectively. Consequently, the unity of office and Electoral College system inhibit development of a multi-party system.

In considering the relationship between the parties and the President a curious paradox has become apparent: whereas the American political party system is a loose coalition, the President's role is pivotal. These two aspects of American political life are reflected throughout the process of Presidential nomination and campaigning, with their attendant liabilities and assets for an aspirant to that office.

Nomination

The process of Presidential nomination has undergone three major changes during the course of American history, the last of which has accelerated during the 1960's and seems likely to continue in the foreseeable future. These changes have moved nomination out of the hands of the Electoral College to a party caucus in Congress, and from there to national party nominating conventions dominated by state and local organizations. Recently, state and local party leaders have been challenged for control of the process by public opinion.

Since the 1830's the national convention system has been used to nominate each party's Presidential and Vice-Presidential candidates and to prepare a national party platform. Every four years Democrats and Republicans in each state choose delegates to their respective national conventions by a variety of means which may include choice by state party committees, state conventions, primaries, or a combination of two or more of these methods, such as the selection of some state delegates by primary elections and others by state party committees. Except for party national committeemen no other individuals may go as delegates, not even United States Senators or Congressmen if they have not been specifically chosen by their states. Thus, delegates to a national convention represent only state and local interests. By the rules of both parties, they are seated and cast their ballots as a state delegation. As a result of this practice, throughout most of American history no man could be nominated for President without the support of state party leaders. At times their control was so great that they could choose dark horse candidates previously unknown to the general public, in the proverbial smoke-filled rooms of the bosses.

However, three twentieth-century changes have made popular support a necessary attribute for Presidential nomination: Presidential preference primaries, public opinion polls, and television. Primaries were a reform initiated by the Progressives to enable the public to express their preferences among candidates and to select delegates to the national conventions. The number of states holding primaries has varied greatly over time, as has the degree to which preferences expressed by the voters have bound state delegates. Nevertheless, primaries do provide a means of testing public reaction to candidates and issues. While not necessarily conclusive in themselves, a strong series of primary victories or several losses can limit the discretion available to delegates at the national convention. The day of the dark horse is over.

During the 1950's the sampling techniques used in public opinion polls became sufficiently sophisticated to be a generally reliable tool of predicting preferences and assessing the public image of any candidate. As refinements continue to be made in the technique, it becomes increasingly possible to gain an accurate image of public reaction to issues, events, and men and to pinpoint differences within the public based on factors such as age, geography, race, income, education, religion, and ethnic background. Television's capacity to communicate quickly and widely both the image of public figures and public opinion trends reinforces the effect of primaries and polls.

Primaries, polls, and television limit the discretion of state and local party leaders in nominating a Presidential candidate, because their goal is winning an election. If the public clearly indicates likes or dislikes, delegates will be guided by this preference as a matter of expediency. However, they have not become rubber stamps because primaries and polls may not provide a clear indication of popular sentiment. When the results of primaries are inconclusive, as they were for Republicans in 1964, or when the polls show a deeply divided public, as in 1968, delegates have greater leeway in the selection process. Consequently, in order to gain his party's nomination, it is necessary for a contemporary candidate to combine support by state party leaders with popular support. Neither alone is sufficient.

Presidential nominations during the 1960's demonstrate the significance of these trends. In 1960 the major Democratic aspirants were John F. Kennedy, Lyndon Johnson, and Hubert Humphrey. The Republican contenders were Richard Nixon and Nelson Rockefeller. The Kennedy campaign clearly demonstrated the reciprocal relationship between support by state and local party leaders and the public.[12] By skillfully attracting some state leaders, and skillfully handling some state Democratic organizations, John Kennedy was able to wage successful primary campaigns. Those successes, in turn, provided a popular bandwagon effect, which aided him in attracting other state leaders and Democratic organizations. Lyndon Johnson was supported by a number of state leaders but entered no primaries and therefore could not demonstrate public support. After the Wisconsin and West Virginia primaries Hubert Humphrey lacked both. On the Republican side, Richard Nixon combined popular support in primaries with the overwhelming support of state leaders. Nelson Rockefeller lacked support among the leadership and chose not to enter primaries. Thus, he posed no real threat to Nixon's nomination.

Four years later Barry Goldwater's advisers were forced to acknowledge the increasing significance of public support. While they would have preferred to have worked solely by capturing state party machinery, they felt obliged to enter the primary battle.[13] The Republican primaries proved inconclusive in 1964, with New Hampshire going to Henry Cabot Lodge, Oregon to Nelson Rockefeller, and California to Barry Goldwater. Thus, in the face of a divided public opinion state party leaders were free to make the decision. They were primarily in favor of Goldwater, who had earned their gratitude through years of service in raising party funds.

In 1964 the Democratic nominee, Lyndon Baines Johnson, was especially favored by being an incumbent President. The audience outside the convention provides incumbent Presidents with a particular advantage in retaining their party's nomination. Due to the growth of mass media focusing public attention on the national level, those involved in the process of delegate selection cannot afford to ignore a President of their party. It is identified with his programs, successes, and failures. To ignore or oppose him is to give ammunition to the opposition party. Repudiation of an incumbent President would repudiate his party's four years of power, destroy the advantages of incumbency, and badly split his party. Therefore, such a repudiation would probably assure victory for the opposition. There are more positive grounds, however, for renominating him. A President receives unparalleled publicity. He can dominate public opinion polls and thus organization support. For example, despite the fact that the vast majority of editorial opinion in the country opposed Harry Truman's reelection in 1948, he was President, and what he did made news. Editorial pages could denounce the candidate, but front page photographs showed the President engaged in activities close to the heart of the voter: signing a bill to extend veterans' aid, inaugurating a local public works project, or conferring with the Chiefs of Staff. Personal characteristics that appealed to the voter as endearingly human qualities also helped to counteract editorial opposition: his obvious affection for his wife, his lively taste in sports shirts, his avid defense of his daughter's voice against music critics.[14] Besides dominating the news, a President can dominate prime evening time on television and radio for a "fireside chat." This gives him priceless national coverage and public attention that are unavailable to any other candidate, no matter how well financed his campaign. Especially in an election year, the President's State of the Union message can do much to shape the events and atmosphere of the campaign. No other public figure in America shares his ability to define the issues and to command the nation's attention for his response to them. Because of the character of American political response (which is more aware of the words and actions of a party in power than of the promises of the opposition), the contemporary incumbent is assured renomination and is favored for reelection if he avoids major political disaster.

In 1968 the Republican contenders for nomination were Richard Nixon and Nelson Rockefeller. The major Democratic aspirants included Lyndon Johnson, Eugene McCarthy, Robert F. Kennedy, and Hubert Humphrey. Nixon combined the support of most of his party's state leaders with an impressive sweep of primary victories, whereas Rockefeller again lacked both. Instead, his strategy emphasized a great showing at the polls to convince party leaders that he was the only Republican candidate who could defeat Democrats for the election. Although poll results generally confirmed this belief, the margins were always too narrow to overcome Nixon's substantial advantage. By his Vietnamese War policy President Johnson provided the major political disaster that destroyed the advantages of incumbency. Apparently fearing a divided party and public repudiation on Election Day, he withdrew quite late in the race. Senator McCarthy faced the problem of any contender against his party's incumbent. By repudiating its leader's policies he split the party and therefore was not widely successful in building support among state party leaders. While he scored some impressive primary victories, Robert Kennedy's belated entry into the race split the opposition to Johnson policies, thus cutting into McCarthy's popular support. Especially after Johnson's April withdrawal from the race, Robert Kennedy built greater support among state party leaders than did McCarthy. At the close of the June primaries in California and South Dakota, Kennedy seemed to have started a bandwagon that would carry him beyond all other contenders in public support, but this promise was cut short by an assassin's bullet. Hubert Humphrey was not a candidate until President Johnson's withdrawal and was therefore not represented in most state primaries. His poll standings showed him slightly behind McCarthy among the general electorate but favored over McCarthy among Democrats. Since both contenders were favored over Nixon in national polls, McCarthy's lead there was insignificant. In 1968 it was unusually difficult to turn public opinion data into a concrete choice at the Democratic Convention. Opinion polls and primaries proved overwhelming support for the combined critics of the administration as opposed to President Johnson, but the convention had to choose between the least popular of the critics and a man who was not Lyndon Johnson. Consequently, in the face of inconclusive public sentiment, Hubert Humphrey's greater support among state party leaders was decisive.

The audience outside the convention may not have appeared to have had a great impact upon the Democratic party's choice of a Presidential candidate in 1968, but several highly significant changes of rules were made which assure broader public participation in 1972. It was decided to require that all delegates be selected within the calendar year of the national convention. (Previously, many states selected delegates as much as two years in advance of the convention, which isolated them from the public concerns of that year.) It was also decided to end the unit rule in selection of delegates and in convention voting. Consequently, the delegates from a state will now represent the variety of candidate preference within the state and be free to vote for a candidate other than the one chosen by a majority of their delegation. The convention also resolved to broaden public understanding of convention rules by codifying and publishing them prior to 1972. It further determined to give greater scope to a previous requirement that delegations be broadly representative of the voting groups within the state party. Thus, the successful Mississippi and Georgia challenges indicated the end of a process of systematic exclusion of negro voters for convention delegates in many Southern states. Each of these changes will increase the impact of the audience outside the convention on Democratic delegates in 1972.

Several attributes make the American Presidential nominating system unique among democratic nations. Most democracies are parliamentary systems in which the national party leadership exercises continuous control over party programs and the political careers of all who bear the party label. In the decentralized American system national party leaders lack such control. Even in nominating the party's titular national leader, they are at a disadvantage because the major national act of American political parties, the Presidential nominating convention, is organized on a federal basis with delegations chosen to represent state or local interests. A second difference between the American nominating system and others is that it must select a man to fill an office that is itself unique. The President has a variety of contradictory functions thrust upon him which no other national leader must face. For example, he must at the same time be both the symbol of his nation (Chief of State) and a partisan spokesman (Chief of Party), both Voice of the American People and World Leader, both Manager of Prosperity and Commander-in-Chief.[15] A third major difference is that in America there is no accustomed route to power. In a parliamentary system the choice of a Prime Minister is based on long service to the party and promotion through a variety of executive positions in the Cabinet. In several countries, including Great Britain, Prime Ministers also share a similar educational background, which helps to make the governing group homogeneous. In contrast, men selected for Presidential nomination have remarkably diverse educational and political backgrounds. Because of the unique nature of Presidential office, this absence of an accustomed path to power is considered an asset in the American system. The qualities necessary to fill that office adequately are not invariably possessed by party bosses or political pros. Therefore, a more flexible system has developed which may enable Americans to select men who meet the particular needs of an era. Rather than a hierarchical system of apprenticeship, the American system permits lateral entry.

Although this high degree of openness also entails a high risk of accident, there are factors which greatly limit that risk. As we have seen, to receive his party's nomination for President, an individual must come to terms with the decentralized nature of American politics and the increased importance of public opinion. Tactics that rely solely on public support (Kefauver '48, Humphrey '60, Lodge '64, McCarthy or Rockefeller '68) or rely solely on the support of state party leaders (Symington or Meyner '60) are unlikely to be successful. The increasing importance of the audience outside the convention has limited the degree of discretion available to the delegates.[16]

The nomination process has proved an effective tool for demonstrating aspects of a man's character which are relevant to successful Presidential performance, including his judgment under fire and his capacity to attract able men and use their ideas effectively and to unite factions within his own party. The President must continually make decisions with inadequate information, under the pressure of deadlines. In this regard, the nomination process provides a valuable indication of his capacity to function well under pressure. Errors of judgment may be indicative of personal characteristics that would produce similar errors in office. For example, in 1960 Hubert Humphrey's impulsive last minute decision to enter the West Virginia primary, contrary to the advice of friends and associates, gave that primary its significance as the beginning of John F. Kennedy's bandwagon. Without Humphrey, Kennedy could not have proved that a Catholic could beat a Protestant in the Bible Belt, which was his major obstacle in gaining the support of party leaders. In 1964 Barry Goldwater's errors of judgment consistently hampered the work of an efficient team of advisers. In the early rounds of the nomination process no one could keep him from making ill-advised statements that were aid and comfort to his enemies. What he *said* about ending social security and defoliating trees in Vietnam with atomic weapons hurt him in the New Hampshire primary and later, despite interminable explanations of what he *meant*.

The nominating process tests more than an individual's judgment under maximum political pressure. It also demonstrates his capacity to attract able men and use their ideas effectively. This is a relevant concern for the President because no man fills the office unaided. No matter how much he might like to run his show alone, he is dependent on his aides, Secretaries, and the whole complex bureaucracy for information, policy formulation, support for his policies on Capitol Hill and with the interest groups, and for carrying out his directives. The key men (his staff, Secretaries, and the upper echelon of the bureaucracy) are appointed by him. Therefore, he must have the capacity to attract able men to Washington. This is difficult unless they are convinced that he is a man of vision and ability who desires the type of policy they do, will give them adequate opportunity for initiative, and will make use of the advice they can give. This attribute is well tested throughout the entire nominating process. No recent candidate has exhibited it to better advantage than John F. Kennedy. The leading lawyers, professors, and businessmen who came to his aid in every state were not on payroll. The level of talent he could gather around him for strategy sessions, speech writing, and organizing local campaign groups came through shared goals and personal loyalty, and was invaluable. Lyndon Johnson could not command that level of personal loyalty from that quality of individual in that quantity. This was demonstrated in his nomination attempt in 1960 and was a serious weakness of his Presidency.[17]

More than attracting able men, a President has to have the capacity to use them effectively and fit them to his style of operation. In 1960 Richard Nixon attracted able men, but often ignored their advice, kept them in ignorance of key decisions, and chose to run a "lone wolf" campaign. Meanwhile, Kennedy demonstrated an ability to use advice well, keeping control of key decisions and effectively delegating power. It has been said that "his intelligence included the ability to know his own limitations of time and knowledge and to draw on the brains of others."[18] Nixon's nomination campaign of 1968 demonstrated that he had learned this valuable lesson and was functioning more smoothly with his staff. Although he still maintained control of most decisions, the lines of communication within his organization were more open, and he used his staff with greater skill and delegated authority effectively.[19]

A candidate's capacity to unite the various factions within his party is another characteristic of political skill tested by the

nominating process. The parties are inevitably divided by geographic and ideological factions that must be skillfully united
by any man who would gain his party's nomination. The whole
process of entering primaries or working with state political
organizations is one in which an individual whose strength lies
in one faction of the party must demonstrate the capacity to
gain the support of other factions. Occasionally, it is possible
for an individual to attain the nomination without this process
if his faction is sufficiently strong, as Goldwater's conservative
supporters were in the 1964 Republican Convention. But in the
convention he must use the one tool available to bind the
factions together if he wishes to campaign with the support of
a united party—a platform that includes planks for all factions.
After refusing the most insignificant changes in party platform,
Goldwater aggravated the situation by selecting a Vice-
Presidential running mate who represented his faction, and
accepting the nomination with his famous "extremism in the
defense of liberty" speech. He left liberal Republicans no home
in his party and paid the consequences on Election Day. There
was a substantial defection of party voters after the convention
for these reasons.[20] It might be said with some justification that
Goldwater lost any chance that his campaign for the Presidency
might have had on the floor of the Cow Palace.

Though long, wearing, expensive, and often undignified, the
American nominating system tests many crucial qualities
relevant to Presidential performance, particularly popular appeal and political skill in handling other political actors and
state party leaders. It demonstrates whether the aspirant has
the capacity to attract able men and use their ideas effectively,
and how he responds under fire. Without these skills no man
would be adequate in the office. Therefore, it has been suggested
that within the limits of American institutions the parties have
evolved a functional nominating system which acknowledges
the decentralization of national politics.[21] A leading analyst of
the nomination process lists three assets of the system: it contributes to the unity and conciliation of both a diverse population and of many party factions; it provides a flexible means
for circulation of leadership and recruitment of candidates; and
it promotes an effective democratic choice between competitive
party leadership.[22]

While this may be generally true, some qualifications and reservations seem relevant. The skills that are tested by the nomination process are domestic. Americans have devised no means to test a candidate's capacity to deal with foreign relations or questions of defense, both of which are key aspects of Presidential activity. Moreover, the system provides no guarantees of success. There are exigencies and contingencies that cannot be controlled, such as the death of a key participant or the lack of available men with adequate political skill and vision to deal with new problems. The field from which a choice must be made is not invariably broad or well supplied with talent. One further reservation is based on the degree to which the politics of the nomination process may function as a later limitation on a winner. Throughout months of hectic activity prior to nomination, an individual must make many policy commitments, deals, or promises which are likely to affect his policies as President. A wise man tries to avoid as many commitments as possible, but he thereby runs the risk of appearing bland, stupid, indecisive, or wily. Despite his better judgment, however, he will be forced into commitments on policies or positions in his administration as part of the give and take of the nomination process, or such commitments will be made in his name by advisers or friends. Either way, he can be limited during his campaign as well as in office. The politics of the campaign process force further concessions and commitments.

Campaigning

After Labor Day the official Presidential campaign begins. It has two purposes: to activate party workers and to motivate the electorate. All the factors that were discussed above—party decentralization, low public interest and partisanship, and the significance of television coverage of a candidate—plus the vast size of the nation, determine the manner in which it must be conducted. They assure that its pace will be inhuman, it will be long, loud, often undignified, and occasionally vicious in personal attack, and it will frequently stress candidate images rather than issues.

Americans are partisan in the sense that they identify with a particular party, but they generally have trouble sorting out the policies for which that party is responsible. In a parlia-

mentary system, partisan debate in the legislature and partisan
formation of public policy maintain a high level of partisanship
throughout the electorate. A party proposes to do something
in its platform; when elected it enacts laws to carry out the
pledge; and later it can be held responsible for the consequences.
Because decentralized parties result in bipartisan support for
major policies, the Presidential campaign must activate the
electorate through long, often violent campaign oratory. This
is underscored by the great size of the country and its large
population.

The campaign process entails two distinct, often conflicting
responsibilities for the Presidential candidate: he must both
activate the party rank and file to work for his election, and
he must motivate the electorate to go to the polls and select
him.[23] The low level of public interest and knowledge concerning politics makes it necessary to activate the party workers
to get out the vote. If, as the leading study of American voters
has indicated, more Americans (seventeen per cent) vote for a
President on the basis of no issue content whatsoever than on
the basis of careful consideration of the issues in the campaign
(fifteen per cent), then the personal, door-to-door contact of
precinct workers with unmotivated or undecided voters may
mean the winning margin in an election. Given the highly
competitive nature of national elections, the extra margin
provided by voters who have turned out primarily because an
active local party organization encouraged them to do so may
be crucial.

No candidate can afford to assume that members of his party
will automatically campaign for his election. Thus, a major part
of his attention and energy must be devoted to his party workers.
The difficulty lies in the fact that in a decentralized party system
the national party has no way to command the support and
activity of its constituent units (the state and local parties).
Whereas parliamentary systems give considerable disciplinary
control to the national party leaders, Americans rely upon the
voluntary enthusiasm of the rank and file. It is a remarkable
political phenomenon that every four years such a diverse group
of people is brought to perceive themselves as part of the same
enterprise without any coercive mechanism. Lacking coercion,

a Presidential candidate is forced to emphasize party symbols by highly partisan statements. For Democrats this means hauling out the banner of the New Deal and blaming Republicans for the Great Depression. For Republicans it means hauling out Abraham Lincoln and traditional symbols of rugged individualism. However, this rhetoric on the part of both parties is distasteful to a good part of the less partisan electorate and must be handled skillfully if the candidate is not to alienate middle-of-the-road voters, independents, and marginal members of the opposition party whom he is anxious to attract.

While the need to activate party workers affects the type of appeals which a Presidential candidate will make, it also affects the physical organization of his campaign. He must travel extensively for this purpose. Briefly, once every four years, representatives of the *states* meet in a Republican or Democratic national nominating convention and select a Presidential and Vice-Presidential candidate. Then they go home, leaving their choices to fend for themselves, which they must do by activating the party workers *in the states*. A great pep-talk from a television studio in New York will have less effect on the party workers in Ohio, Texas, or California than a personal visit. Despite the marvels of television, those workers must be activated to get out the vote in their respective states by personal appearances. Improvements in transportation have greatly shortened distances, but that has not eased the campaign burden. While jet travel has ended the old whistle-stop tour on a Presidential "special" train, it encourages men to make a breakfast speech in Boston, a luncheon speech in Chicago, a five o'clock speech in Salt Lake City, and address an evening rally in Los Angeles, with interspersed conferences with local political leaders in cars, planes, elevators, or hotel rooms. The need to reach party workers at the state level and the huge size of the nation make long campaigns inevitable.

The low level of ideology in the country assures that personality factors will be stressed over ideological ones. This is always an invitation for violent, vindictive oratory and for stress on image instead of issue. The vicious quality of a campaign can be controlled by a candidate if he takes a firm stand, as Nixon did against any attempts by his supporters to activate religious bigotry in the 1960 campaign. But more significant as a limit on viciousness than good manners, taste, or decency is the potential for vicious rhetoric to backfire. Two of the great handicaps of the Goldwater campaign were his frightening statements and some of his more violent supporters, both of which drove many Republicans to support Lyndon Johnson.

The stress on image is difficult to avoid because the medium used for communication affects the message. Through the 1930's and 1940's the primary medium of political communication was the radio; since the 1950's it has been television. Each of these media requires different skills. Radio is a method of aural communication to which most people listen as an accompaniment to other activities. To sustain interest, a political candidate must have a good speaking voice and excellent organization and wit. Television, on the other hand, is primarily a method of visual communication. The image sustains the interest. The contrast between the two was best demonstrated in the 1952 campaign. It was the first Presidential campaign in which television played a significant part, yet television was sufficiently new so that there were several areas without reception. This situation enabled analysts to see the different impact of the candidates through the media.[24] His frequent pauses and murky syntax hurt General Eisenhower's radio delivery. In those areas which relied on radio communication, the study just cited found that he did poorly when opposed to Stevenson's skillful use of the medium. Television was another matter. Balding, bespectacled, and round-shouldered, Stevenson opposed the image of a vigorous man of action with military dash and fatherly presence. (Appropriately enough, Stevenson's campaign symbol was a shoe with a hole in the sole.) Thus, in areas where television was the main medium of communication, Stevenson was less successful than Eisenhower.

In later campaigns the parties came to terms with the medium. Political candidates for most important offices now look as though they and their families were supplied by central casting. They are generally presented in brief "spots" like commercials, less because the medium is expensive than because audience attention is extremely limited. This inattention makes it unwise for campaigns to attempt to educate the public. Rather, they are most effective when they aim at reinforcing partisan biases.[25]

Perhaps the greatest defect of campaigns is that they entail a tremendous expenditure of time and money. Since no one knows what works, everything is tried in the greatest quantity possible from winking buttons and comic book biographies to telethons and huge rallies.[26]

Given these drawbacks, one may justifiably ask whether campaigns test Presidential capacity in any way. The answer is mixed. Many significant aspects are certainly tested. While all of these have been tested previously in the nominating process, the campaign period brings them into sharper focus.

Like the nominating process, campaigns test a candidate's political skill, including his ability to work with other political actors and his ability to grasp the "political facts of life," making the best use of his resources. Kennedy in 1960, Johnson in 1964, and Nixon in 1968 were proficient in this. In 1960 Nixon was weak on both counts. He chose a lone wolf campaign that kept Eisenhower on the sidelines until it was too late and stubbornly refused to change plans to visit all fifty states despite the fact that this left him in Alaska during the crucial final phase when Kennedy was stumping the industrial centers. In 1964 Goldwater alienated a large proportion of his party's leadership and voters by ignoring basic political realities. In 1968 Humphrey proved unable to unite his party. As a result, major party leaders and many rank-and-file workers devoted their energies to local and state campaigns rather than the Presidential one.

Like the nomination process, campaigns test the capacity of a candidate to attract able men to his service and to use their advice intelligently. They test a candidate's ability to unify a nation through skillful consensus building. They also test a man's personal qualities under stress. In the campaign process the electorate learned that Truman was a fighter who would not accept defeat, that Dewey was overconfident, that Stevenson's integrity and wit could not compensate for a basic incapacity to take decisive action under the unrelieved pressure of political events, that in 1960 Nixon grew morose and moody under pressure, that Kennedy could "keep his cool," that by 1968 Nixon had learned how to play a winning hand, and that Humphrey was impetuously garrulous.

Valuable as these indications of a man's Presidential potential may be, there are several major weaknesses in the campaign process. As was the case with the nomination process, campaigns test only domestic skills. Their emphasis on image clouds any indication of the candidate's intellectual competence. Furthermore, a campaign can indicate capacities but there is no assurance that in office the candidate will apply these skills appropriately. Kennedy, for example, showed great political skill in campaigning but not in the passage of his legislation. Finally, the effectiveness of campaigns depends on the effectiveness of the nomination process. If that process accomplishes its function of producing a candidate who can demonstrate popular and political skill and unify a party, the campaign will provide an opportunity to test him under conditions of close opposition. If, however, it produces a Goldwater, his opponent will not be adequately tested as he will not face significant competition. For example, the sensitivity to criticism and difficulty in attracting able men to his service were weaknesses in Johnson which were obscured because he lacked a really competitive opposition. Johnson merely had to appear strong and comforting and allow Goldwater to frighten the electorate into his arms. Similarly, the 1968 campaign did not prove whether Nixon had reformed, because Humphrey's campaign was not an adequate challenge. It began late and had such serious organizational problems that Humphrey was on the defensive throughout. In summary, the campaign process is a fairly effective mechanism for eliminating candidates with major flaws, but it does not *assure* good Presidential performance.

Preparing for Office
Once elected, an individual has two months in which to prepare to assume Presidential office. Hundreds of important decisions must be made, and a mass of information absorbed. The President-elect must first learn as much as he can from the outgoing administration about the policies for which he will become responsible, particularly in defense and foreign affairs. Though

this would seem to be a natural part of the transition of power, no statute or regulation governs it. It is simply an act of courtesy on the part of the departing President. While some limited attempts were made earlier, the practice began in its contemporary form under Harry Truman. Few men have been as intimately aware of the problems and dangers inherent in ascending to the Presidency without information on the secret military and diplomatic plans in which the government was involved. As Vice-President he had been almost completely ignored by President Roosevelt. On Roosevelt's death Truman suddenly found himself responsible for decisions on the final phase of the Second World War and the development of atomic weapons, about which he had known little. This crash indoctrination convinced him that his successor should be given adequate briefing sessions on all important areas of policy in each of the departments. Eisenhower continued and elaborated the practice, which has come to be expected of every President. It has come to include briefings of the new Cabinet appointees as well. Some limited briefings were even given to candidates during the 1960, 1964, and 1968 Presidential campaigns. In 1960 the two candidates appointed personal representatives to meet with experts on the transition problem under the auspices of the Brookings Institution.[27]

A related series of activities which crowds this brief period involves preparing the new President's program. This includes setting up a personal staff, establishing study groups and brain trusts, meeting with key figures in and out of government, and writing the Inaugural Address, which outlines his program. While the campaign has defined much of his program, there is a great deal of work left to be done on organization, resolution of conflicting commitments, and planning the best strategies to attain his goals. Moreover, the President is responsible for a staggering breadth and detail of policy. While some brain trusts and study committees are established by candidates for office with an eye to these future problems, the demands of campaigning tend to syphon off most of the talent and energy of the able men he can enlist. Therefore, a great deal of work must be done quickly after election.

A personal staff is usually easy to organize because the

nomination and campaign process has proved a testing ground for his associates and advisers and has helped him to develop a personal "team." It has also given him an indication of whose help would be best for study groups and all advisory functions. The Inaugural Address is a project to which he and many of his staff must devote great attention because it is here that the key themes of his Presidency will be presented, here that his distinctive signature must show. The address may be the work of many speech writers, but it requires constant supervision on his part.

Meeting key public and private figures has a symbolic and substantive purpose. Symbolically, he must assure the various interests, groups, and leaders throughout the country that he will be President of all. He must also bind factional wounds created during the campaign and show proper appreciation of his supporters. There is also a substantive purpose for these meetings. Hardly any man's acquaintance is broad enough to encompass all the major aspects of American life. For example, John F. Kennedy was well acquainted with the leaders of the intellectual community but knew few business leaders before becoming President. Lyndon Johnson was well acquainted with Congressional and bureaucratic leaders but had little acquaint-ance with the intellectual community or many state party leaders. Eisenhower's acquaintance was primarily with military and business leaders. Each man had to become acquainted with a broader spectrum of American leadership in order to try to attract their loyalty, or at least allay hostility, gather ideas for formulating his programs, and find men to appoint to the hundreds of positions for which a President is responsible.

This suggests a third major activity of the transition stage—appointments. Every President-elect must appoint a complete Cabinet, many under-secretaries, key staff and diplomatic personnel, plus men to fill vacancies that may be created through resignation or normal expiration of term of office. This process will be closely scrutinized by the press and political cognoscenti with the attention of pagan priests searching the entrails of birds for their omen. What he does, omits, or is rumored to have done or omitted will help to create the first impression of his likely capacity in office. It is a time above all when he is on his mettle to show those political skills of coalition building which are necessary for pluralistic American society. Therefore, selection of men for these offices has increasingly been based on factors of experience and specialized competence rather than party membership or service.[28]

Throughout these hectic days the President-elect must also rest and prepare himself psychologically for the Presidency. The physical and emotional strain of the nomination and campaign process have been punishing for all concerned. Both staff and President-elect need a vacation, but time is a luxury when there is so much to do in two months. Therefore, only the briefest rest is allowed, which usually includes preliminary work on several of the areas previously discussed. Psychological preparation is equally difficult. In other political systems leaders are given more preparation for their roles. Monarchs have been trained from childhood, Prime Ministers have been prepared through a series of Cabinet posts, but in America a man can be propelled into the Presidency from private life or a lower political office that lacked either executive or national experience. Habits of a lifetime must be changed by him and his family once he is elected and the Secret Service comes to stay. Perhaps no man feels his inadequacy for this incredible office so intensely as one who has just attained it.

These few weeks pass quickly, and in the miserable cold of mid-winter the man who has gone through so much already is inaugurated, to face the Presidential paradox.

II. Changing Responsibilities

WHEN A CONTEMPORARY President-elect swears on Inauguration Day that he will "faithfully execute the office of President of the United States," he assumes responsibility for an office that has been substantially altered since the 1930's by the impact of two trends, routinization and institutionalization.

"Routinization" means that the bold innovations of each President become actions whose performance is *expected* of any President as a matter of custom or routine. His various constituencies (electoral, congressional, bureaucratic, party, press, interest group or international) expect and come to require that form of initiative from him. Virtually all the *ad hoc* innovations associated with strong Presidents have been routinized within the last three decades by custom and statute. This has led to changes in the President's relationship with the public, Congress, and his party, and greatly increased his economic, foreign, and defense responsibilities.

Routinization has led to "institutionalization"—the development of groups or individuals organized for the purpose of assisting the President to provide those services that are routinely expected of him. Naturally, institutions have proliferated with the accelerated growth of expectations for Presidential services.

The following pages are devoted to an analysis of the changing responsibilities that the President has been given and the institutional support that has come with them.

CHANGING RELATIONSHIP WITH THE PUBLIC

Technological developments have provided the President with invaluable new means to reach the public directly and continually and to receive accurate information on the nature of public response. These developments have, however, also enabled groups within the public to have a direct means of access to the same broad audience if they can develop appropriate techniques to capture media attention. Moreover, the central role in public consciousness which the President has attained makes him the natural focus of any group desiring change. Therefore, the changing nature of his relationship with the public must provide a mixed blessing for any President.

Changing Means of Communication

The low level of interest and attention to party politics and public events in America provides a President with an important asset over his opposition. It has been found that "In the electorate as a whole the level of attention to politics is so low that what the public is exposed to must be highly visible—even stark—if it is to have an impact on opinion."[1] The President has a greater capacity to dramatize events than any other political actor. His unique position as a nationally elected official, the excitement and interest inherent in his office, and his opportunities to use the mass media in press conferences and fireside chats are invaluable assets if used skillfully. However, his advantage over others is one of degree. He too has trouble breaking through the general indifference. Furthermore, that same exposure may also be a liability for a President who does not use the media intelligently by taking into consideration his audience, his opposition, the nature of the media, and his personal assets and liabilities in its use. To be effective, a President must find a style of media use which is consistent with his personal capacity. As the pace of routinization accelerates, the type of demands made on Presidents in their use of the mass media becomes increasingly restrictive. Nevertheless, the benefits to be derived can amply repay a President for the effort involved in media use. These benefits, the accelerating pace of routinization and institutionalization, and their attendant restrictions are demonstrated by the changing ways in which Presidents have tried to relate to the mass media as they have become more complex.

Revolutionary technical changes in the media have posed

problems for Presidents but have also transformed the office. The three great Presidential innovators in use of the mass media were Theodore Roosevelt for newspapers, Franklin Roosevelt for radio, and John F. Kennedy for television.[2]

Prior to the 1890's newspapers had been small-circulation party organs, but the development of means for rapid, inexpensive printing made a mass market both possible and necessary. This in turn contributed to a growing public awareness of governmental activities and personnel. For many reasons, including its unity, continuous activity, and dependence on personal characteristics of the man in office, the Presidency was well adapted for human interest stories, which were, and continue to be, a staple of newspaper reporting. Realizing the significance of press coverage for Presidential leadership, Theodore Roosevelt seized the initiative and actively and continually used every means at his disposal to achieve favorable press coverage. Symbolically, he was the first President to provide room in the White House for the press. Woodrow Wilson inaugurated mass press conferences during his early years and attempted to exploit the press until the First World War. Thereafter he attempted, with varying degrees of success, to go over their heads to the people, but the technology of his day made this difficult and time consuming. His successors, Warren Harding and Calvin Coolidge, continued the practice of press conferences which became routinely expected of all succeeding Presidents. Those were small, formal meetings in which the press had to submit questions in advance, enabling the President to prepare an answer.

Franklin Roosevelt's press conference was a considerable innovation in regularity and format. It was held twice weekly in the Oval Room of the White House with the regular, accredited White House correspondents who still composed a relatively small group of men. He dropped the written question and answer, substituting direct questioning and three categories of answer: on the record, background, and off the record. In their articles reporters would directly quote the President's "on the record" answers. They could use the material given to them in a "background" answer, but not attribute it to the President. (It would usually be attributed to some euphemism like "a reliable source" or a "high official source.") Information given "off the record" could not be reported.

The liabilities of this format for the President were the basic liabilities of any press conference. His weakness or ignorance might be exposed. He might give ill considered or ill phrased answers. Above all, he had to expect a good share of hostile or negative reporting because newspapers cannot sell copy unless they can stir interest, which is hard to do with headlines on the level of "once again, the President was wonderful." In publishing, good news is not news. Even as distinguished a newspaper as *The New York Times* seemed to President Kennedy guilty of unnecessary hostility. He was reportedly unable to understand "how its editors could agree with 90 percent of his program and still write what at times seemed to him 90 percent unfavorable editorials."[3]

Nevertheless, as they were used by Franklin Roosevelt, press conferences filled two important functions:

> First, they served as a forum from which to discuss pending policies and urge their favorable consideration in Congress, or build support in the country that in turn would be translated into pressure on the legislature. But the conferences were also a means of conveying the presidential image to the country, keeping interest in the White House and the doings of its occupant at a high pitch, and thus helping to maintain the public as a receptive audience for more specific appeals.[4]

The conferences thus enabled a President to place his own interpretation on events and policies, which helped to inform and influence subsequent debate on the issue. To assure that the matters about which he was concerned were brought up, President Roosevelt occasionally resorted to the use of "planted" questions, a practice followed by all of his successors. Debate, therefore, occurred on *his* terms, and he could choose to present his ideas in their most favorable light where they would receive the widest coverage. As has been noted, other political actors were thus placed at a disadvantage because they would generally receive less media coverage and less public attention.

These advantages of the Rooseveltian press conference have continued to the present day, but he had other advantages that his successors do not share, due to technological developments. Roosevelt's format had the added advantage of a testing ground of ideas on men and on the public. He used background and off the record answers frequently and imaginatively. He could send up trial balloons under the background disguise, and if they were shot down by public reaction, he was not committed to carrying out the policy, nor would he lose face by being seen to retreat under fire. Background answers were thus a very useful way to sample public opinion on an individual issue. The off the record answer could be used to brief members of the press on policies or actions which could not safely be disclosed at that time (especially during war). It sought to minimize "irresponsible" criticism of governmental action and was a way to test out ideas on members of the press corps. It further served to educate newsmen on complex matters of governmental policy, which helped to assure more informed reporting.

Franklin Roosevelt also placed his unique stamp upon radio, a relative newcomer to the mass media. His predecessors from Calvin Coolidge had simply used radio as an adjunct to speeches. They had dealt with a live audience and merely allowed radio to carry their words to a broader one. Unlike his predecessors, Franklin Roosevelt realized the dual significance of radio use for a President. First, the medium required entirely different techniques from those appropriate to other types of public speaking because the audience was far more diverse and elusive than any other. However, radio had the distinct advantage of allowing a President to bypass and supplement the printed news media. *If* in his use of the medium the President was sufficiently skillful to be able to capture his audience's attention, that audience would receive his message as it was sent, rather than through the filter of newspaper reporting. The particular importance of this for a Democratic President was not lost on Franklin Roosevelt. He well knew that as newspapers had become large-scale businesses and were dependent upon the business community for advertising revenue they were generally Republican in editorial policy. This fact has affected every Democratic aspirant for Presidential office and every Democratic President from Roosevelt's day to the present. For example, statistics on editorial support for Democratic Presidential candidates indicate a high of only twenty-three per cent for Roosevelt in 1940 and a low of fifteen per cent for Stevenson in 1952 and Kennedy in 1960.[5] The majority of support achieved by Lyndon Johnson in 1964 was less a demonstration of change of editorial policy than a reaction to the unusual nature of his opposition and is unlikely to be repeated.

Franklin Roosevelt had an excellent radio presence and developed the format of a "fireside chat" to maximize his influence on public opinion. This was a report to the people by the President on a matter of grave public importance at an evening hour. He used it to report, review, and explain as well as to build public morale. His was a "soft sell" technique of conversing with the American people which made maximum use of the medium's potential for persuasion and image building. Few other political actors on the American scene had his skill, and none could command as wide a coverage or audience over as continuous a period as could the President. The development of the electronic era was beginning to have its impact on the Presidential office.

Roosevelt's successors, Harry Truman and Dwight Eisenhower, were not as adept in use of the media, either in press conferences or radio coverage. Neither had as effective a delivery, nor Roosevelt's great zest for public relations, yet both were compelled to continue his practices because public and press expectations had become routinized. They therefore were forced to develop formats more appropriate to their capacities.

Partially as a matter of necessity, Harry Truman chose to formalize the press conference. He cut the biweekly meetings to one, transferred its locale from the White House to the Indian Treaty Room of the Old State Department Building, permitted an enlarged attendance, and conducted the meetings in a formal manner. This ended the easy rapport and casual banter between press and President and turned the press conference into a semi-public performance. He also cut use of the fireside chat but never attempted to develop an appropriate formula for the new medium of television, which was rapidly supplanting radio. Uncritically and unreflectively he accepted it as merely an adjunct to radio.[6]

Dwight Eisenhower was even less enthusiastic about press conferences than Harry Truman had been. Therefore, President

Eisenhower further reduced the number of scheduled conferences, especially after his illness, and made them even more
public and formal. His advisers were, however, aware of the
significance of television. Although he was unable to use that
medium as skillfully as his successor, he recognized the need
for expert assistance in dealing with its complexities. Therefore,
in addition to his Press Secretary, James Hagerty, he relied on
the actor Robert Montgomery as a special assistant and adviser
for television coverage, and occasionally turned to the advertising company of Batten, Barton, Durstine, and Osborn to write
and produce some of his more elaborate vehicles.[7]

The medium of television was fully mastered for Presidential
use by John F. Kennedy. He had both zest for and skill in using
it as a source of direct, unmediated, instantaneous, and massive
access to the public.[8] He used a variety of techniques and
formats for the fireside chat and transformed the press conference into a totally public meeting, in which the press merely
provided an excuse for a meeting in which the President used
television to reach beyond them to the public. He chose to move
the press conference to the auditorium of the New State Department Building, enlarged the membership, and allowed live
television coverage of the event. Before questions were permitted, President Kennedy made any announcements that he
particularly desired to present to the public. His preparation
for the conferences was elaborate, enabling him to answer
effectively on an extemporaneous basis.[9] He used these conferences vigorously to build public support for his policies
and to maintain legislative leadership by discussing his preferences on pending Congressional action or indicating actions that
he intended to request. Thus, in Kennedy's administration, the
press conference and fireside chat merged as a means to reach
the public directly. Nevertheless, the press was not forgotten.
President Kennedy also devised a number of successful ways
to reach reporters with background information, such as special
press conferences with the Press Secretary, Pierre Salinger, and
issuance of advance texts of all speeches or background information on issues that concerned the President.

Prior to 1968 Richard Nixon's press relations had seemed to
alternate between frigid and stormy, and his television image

was considered poor. During his campaign he worked diligently to soften and humanize the image through the use of humor and glimpses of the private man behind the candidate. He promised an "open Presidency" in terms of making information available to the media and actively courted them in his initial press conferences as President.

Lyndon Johnson demonstrated a similar sensitivity to the importance of television coverage and used messages to Congress such as the Civil Rights message of 1964, the Civil Disobedience message of 1967, or all of his State of the Union messages as an excuse to speak directly to the electorate via television. He also experimented widely with the frequency, style, and format of his press conferences. However, part of this wide experimentation was caused by the fact that he found it difficult to develop a public press conference format that would be as appropriate to his style as Kennedy's format had been. Therefore, the number of press conferences dwindled, and several occurred on what appeared to have been the spur of the moment with White House correspondents panting after the President on a brisk walk through the rose garden. Such a format had the advantage for the President that the only available reporters would be those most dependent on his good will. There was also little time to prepare searching questions.

This brief summary of changing practices in use of the mass media indicates their importance for the contemporary Presidency. The electronic revolution has given the President means to reach the public with unparalleled ease and speed. He has also, as one observer noted, "achieved an omnipresence in the general flow of news and in the awareness of the average citizen which in itself has vast implications for the shaping both of national opinion and of public policy."[10]

Nevertheless, there are also liabilities and frustrations inherent in his preeminent position. These include the interdependent difficulties of breaking through the barriers of public indifference and mastering the media. As has been suggested, the President may have greater exposure than any other political actor, but this does not assure that he will be able to overcome the general public apathy to political events. To do so he must not only develop appropriate technical skills; he must also learn to guard against overexposure, in order to safeguard his capacity to command public attention when needed (as, for example, during the Cuban missile crisis of 1961). It might be said that the impact of a fireside chat has almost an inverse ratio to the frequency with which it is used. If it is used sparingly, it will draw a large audience and therefore have great impact. If it becomes a regular television feature it runs a risk of losing its audience. Given the degree of public apathy on political matters, no President can compete on a regular basis with "I Love Lucy." Recognition of this problem has led to a decreasing use of press conferences and fireside chats since the days of Franklin Roosevelt. He held ninety-two press conferences, Truman held forty-four, and Eisenhower twenty-six.[11] Kennedy held twenty-six in three years, which suggests an increased use, but he maintained a highly selective policy on public exposure, which was described in the following terms: "As a commander saves his biggest guns for the biggest battle, so Kennedy limited his direct national appeals to situations of sufficient importance to demand it and sufficiently fluid to be helped by it."[12]

The problems posed for an individual who would master the media are too complex to handle without expert assistance. Increasingly, therefore, Presidential presentations have become products of the joint efforts of many men. Of these, the best known are those who form part of the White House Staff. This staff provides an example of the fact that institutionalization has been the result of obligations which the public has come to expect of the President during the last three decades.

Until 1937 the President had no formally designated official staff. Rather, he received assistance from staff on departmental payrolls on an *ad hoc* basis. From an early stage personal services were provided such as clerical personnel at times of need or the services of the Army Telegraph Office during the Civil War. By Hoover's Presidency, when requested, the departments also sent people to assist the President in specified areas of policy planning. In Hoover's day the White House Staff was composed of a small clerical staff and one to three personal secretaries. Franklin Roosevelt experienced an unprecedented, continuous deluge of mail, which necessitated rapid expansion of the clerical force, but other pressures also caused such expansion of the

White House Staff that today the small staff Hoover knew has become a body numbering about 2,845 persons, which necessitated adding an East Wing to the White House and converting the nearby Victorian building which had housed three departments (State, War, and Navy) to an Executive Office Building.[13]

Under the impact of these pressures, in 1937 President Roosevelt established a Committee on Administrative Management, under the leadership of Louis Brownlow. Its findings, popularly known as the Brownlow Report, underscored the impossible nature of the Presidential workload and his great need for assistance. These findings were reflected in the Reorganization Act of 1939, which formed the legal basis for Reorganization Plan No. 1 and Executive Order 8248. These established the Executive Office of the President with an expanded White House Office including three secretaries and six administrative assistants. Eventually, this staff grew and key men were given their own staffs to cope with the varied nature of their responsibilities.

Presidents have used many different members of their staff to help them prepare for radio or television coverage. For example, President Kennedy generally held a breakfast or luncheon meeting in preparation for his press conferences at which his aides were expected to pelt him with searching questions and to provide any information he lacked. The White House Staff member who has continuous responsibility for this area is the Press Secretary. His office was established by Franklin Roosevelt as a part of the newly developed Executive Office of the President. Because President Roosevelt held biweekly press conferences and maintained a personal relationship with members of the Washington press corps, it was possible for him, in a very real sense, to be his own press secretary. Nevertheless, Stephen Early was a great asset to him.[14] Harry Truman was far less aware of the significance of media use and consequently paid little personal attention to the subject. Furthermore, he selected and kept a Press Secretary who proved ineffective, Charles Ross.[15] Although Dwight Eisenhower had little taste for cultivating the mass media and few personal ideas on the best means to do so, he was aware of the significance of appropriate media use. Therefore, he selected a Press Secretary of unusual capacity and dedication. James Hagerty handled press relations so completely that he even held his own press conferences. As one scholar has noted:

> Hagerty, in short, worked for a man who was only too glad to leave both the grubby details of public relations and, apparently, much of the high strategy to a subordinate. . . . [Hagerty was] the sole link with the curious world, in times of health as well as sickness.[16]

Because President Kennedy had a personal interest in public relations and had been elected by such a narrow margin, he devoted much personal attention to reporters. Therefore, his Press Secretary, Pierre Salinger, functioned in a different manner than had previous Press Secretaries. His primary concerns were coordination of the various executive agencies to produce an integrated public relations policy for the administration and building the administration's image through "exposing key people from all over the country to the President, to administration officials, and to the major elements of the Kennedy program."[17] To do this Salinger expanded and further developed machinery for issuing press releases and getting background material to the press. The emphasis on public relations led to an expansion of the number of ghost writers, or staff aides who assisted in the preparation of messages of all types. Some specialized in particular areas such as labor, economic affairs, or civil rights, but there was generally a degree of flexibility in their use. President Johnson continued the emphasis of his predecessor.

As has been indicated, the expert assistance that a President needs to use the media well far exceeds the scope of a single Press Secretary or all of his administrative assistants. Ghost writers, voice coaches, advertising agencies, and make-up men have become part of the standard, essential cadre of Presidential assistants. This has led some observers to the conclusion that the President is a product merchandised by others, whose own characteristics are irrelevant. Such an interpretation would be a mistake, however. All aspects of the Presidential office entail reliance on advice and assistance from others, but no man except the President can assemble his advisers, and no man except the President can determine the use or abuse he will make of their advice. Had Harry Truman received far more effective assistance he would still have lacked Kennedy's impact, because he lacked Kennedy's sensitivity to the nuances and importance of appropriate use of the media. In fact, it might be argued that Truman's lack of sensitivity was the reason he did not receive more effective assistance. Only a President who was relatively insensitive on this point would have chosen and kept an ineffective Press Secretary. Although the end result is the product of the labor of many individuals, the President has the difficult job of presenting it in a way that will enhance his personal image.

> The subtleties and difficulties here derive from the overriding importance of presidential personality and skill. . . . He must use intelligently and imaginatively the skills of others. . . . The ultimate test is his ability to do all of this, while at the same time enhancing rather than blurring his *individual* image as the source of initiative and energizer of public policy. His individuality is a key asset which must not become submerged in a collegial effort by hucksters and ghosts.[18]

One further difficulty inherent in use of the mass media is that success depends on invoking the role of national spokesman, symbol, and leader. This is incompatible with his necessary partisan functions, which leads to public disillusionment whenever he takes a partisan stand.

> The vast impact of the mass media in capitalizing on the President as good copy, the President's own exploitation of these possibilities for "image-building," and a general yearning in the public for a nonpartisan national symbol—a yearning reinforced by the anxieties of cold war— have lifted the White House occupant above the sordid arena of partisan politics. Thus, any effort to participate in the party or group struggle, as a President must, is as likely to produce shock and disillusionment as it is to enlist active support.[19]

Neither may this national image necessarily be an effective mechanism for Presidential leverage on Congress, which is organized on the basis of local interests and where a majority of members, including committee chairmen, have safe seats. It is this tension between the national image and partisan or legislative leverage which may partially help to explain President Kennedy's inability to achieve passage of major pieces of his legislative program despite skillful media use.

Twentieth-century changes in the means of communicating with the public parallel changing means of public response to the President. These have gained particular significance during the decade of the 1960's and appear likely to have increasing importance for the exercise of Presidential power in the future.

Changing Means of Public Response

The means through which the public can respond to a President have altered through the development of increasingly sophisticated techniques of sampling public opinion and the development of television as the primary means of political communication in America. Because these changes are of such recent origin, it is difficult adequately to assess their long-term impact. Therefore, they will be discussed only briefly to indicate the nature of the trends, to describe the degree of institutionalization which has developed to meet them, and to evaluate their significance for the contemporary President.

As was discussed in Chapter I, the development of sophisticated techniques for assessing public opinion has substantially altered the nomination process. It has had an equally significant impact on the process of governing. If the appropriate questions are asked, public opinion polls can provide a President with a wide variety of useful information. For example, it is currently possible to discover the issues that concern the public, the depth of public interest and knowledge on a given issue, the rank order of preference among possible solutions, the image a candidate projects, and the reasons for the image. Moreover, it is possible to distinguish subgroups within the general public in order to determine differences in attitude toward issues or individuals which are related to age, sex, race, religion, ethnic background, geographic location, or socio-economic factors. Thus, the new opinion sampling techniques provide a President with a means of directly assessing his standing with the public or particular subgroups within the public, and the degree of awareness and concern about a particular issue. There are limitations on the clarity of this information, due to the problems inherent in polling techniques and the vagueness of opinion on the part of many individuals sampled, but they can be useful guides.

Previously, Presidents had been forced to rely primarily on

advice by "pros," information collected by friends and relatives, or mail analysis. As more attention was paid to the polls, it became routinely expected that the President would be continually aware of their findings and responsive to them. The expectation of Presidential responsiveness developed as a partial consequence of the publicity which polls received in the mass media. Poll results are highlighted in the news. Therefore, the attentive public is made aware of the nature of public opinion and the President's response to it. If he does not respond on important issues, his general image will be damaged. While most voters may be unaware of specific issues or political events, they do gather from the media and local opinion leaders a perception of the President as responsive to the public or the opposite. In fact, a substantial proportion of the Presidential electorate votes on the basis of little more than such images. (Twenty-three per cent vote for a President on the basis of their sense of the "nature of the times" and seventeen per cent vote with no issue content whatsoever.) Thus, the widespread expectation of Presidential responsiveness involves him routinely in gathering public "feedback" in order either to use it as a guide for policy planning, or as a guide to the areas of public thought which he must try to change through the various persuasive techniques at his disposal. In either case, prompt action is required.

The expectation was institutionalized by Kennedy's appointment of Louis Harris to his staff. Harris and a corps of assistants had developed the latest scientific opinion polling techniques which Kennedy used as a form of feedback on the public impact of his speeches and actions. His successor was so concerned for polls that during the first half of his administration he quoted them frequently and was often reported as carrying the latest results with him. President Johnson's enthusiasm was short-lived, however. As time passed, an increasing minority of the public voiced disapproval of his Vietnamese War policy. The critics were divided among those who favored American withdrawal and those who favored escalation of the war, but the President did little to appease either side. Rather, he created an image of an increasingly rigid, unresponsive, and defensive figure on an issue that came to involve most of the nation. While the public was not sufficiently ideological to speak with a clear voice on the manner in which the Vietnamese involvement should be handled, it was sufficiently aware of the issue to show dissatisfaction over the conduct of the war. This dissatisfaction focused on the President, whose responses were inadequate to regain popular support. Thus, within four years the man who won the most resounding electoral victory of the century felt compelled to withdraw from a second campaign for fear of a severe defeat at the hands of the electorate. This dramatically indicates the growing importance of responding effectively to information derived from public opinion polls. The President must either act upon the public's response (or at least give that appearance) or act to change the response itself by persuading the public to see matters in a different light. Given a non-ideological and politically inattentive public, however, there are limits on the degree to which a President can change basic attitudes. Public opinion is rarely sufficiently sophisticated and informed to be able to indicate the means a President must use, but it can indicate the area in which he should act and penalize a failure to respond.[20]

The development of television as the primary means of political communication in America may have provided the President with unparalleled means to reach the public in an unmediated fashion, but it has also given others a far more effective means to capture public attention than ever before. While the President has a greater capacity to dominate the medium over a continuous period, individual groups can plan particularly dramatic demonstrations, which will briefly capture public attention. Such a possibility has led a number of groups to develop techniques designed to focus the attention of television on their cause. The civil rights movement of the 1960's was particularly effective in developing non-violent techniques geared to television's emphasis on images rather than words. Peaceful marches and sit-ins demonstrated the depth of commitment on the part of civil rights workers. Through the violent reaction that followed, the evils which the civil rights movement opposed were given vivid media expression throughout the nation in images of police dogs, cattle prods, hate-filled faces, mob violence, and assassination. Such images created widespread national awareness of the existence of a problem and public sentiment favoring change. Inevitably, that sentiment was articulated as a demand for Presidential action.

This inevitability of a demand for Presidential action is closely related to Presidential use of television. As has been suggested, he is omnipresent in the flow of news and in the awareness of the average citizen. The very fact that he continually invokes the role of national spokesman, symbol, and leader means that he will be the focus of public attention when the public desires change. Thus, for him the medium is a two-edged sword.

From the middle of the 1960's, more violent techniques were used to capture television's attention. Ghetto riots became a major expression of discontent over the slow progress toward equal opportunity.[21] Vietnamese War protesters and groups of the New Left, such as the Students for a Democratic Society, increasingly engaged in confrontation politics to provoke violence and thus benefit from television coverage. Public response to violence often took the form of backlash against the protesters rather than support for their cause, but either reaction tended to focus on the President. Routinely, it was expected that he would act when such events occurred. There might have been no clear indication of what to do, but he was definitely expected to take some kind of action.

Therefore, the President had to institutionalize a wide variety of supporting personnel to fill a dual function: providing symbolic reassurance for the public and providing information and policy alternatives for him. The contemporary President is now surrounded by scores of consultants and task forces. Attempts to reassure the public or particular segments of it have caused him to appoint a number of advisory commissions and hold White House conferences. While all of these measures may assist him in obtaining information and public reassurance, they present two major drawbacks. Presidential time is very limited, and the proliferation of commissions, task forces, conferences, and consultants with which he must meet and with whose reports he must be familiar poses a serious drain on his resources. Of even greater concern to a President is the inevitable potential of these groups to backfire. Advisory commissions may not soothe and reassure the public but rather request reforms that provoke further public controversy, as did the Advisory Com-

mission on Civil Disorders established by President Johnson to
investigate the widespread urban riots of 1967. The President
found this report politically embarrassing because it did not
reassure the public that he had already done a great deal in
the area, nor did it call for reforms that he felt were feasible
given the mood of the country. Therefore, little mention was
ever made by the President of the report. Nevertheless, his
reticence did not end the public expectation that he would act.
Similar problems were caused by the White House conferences
on Civil Rights, International Cooperation Year, and Eric
Goldman's Festival of the Arts. During the last two years of
his Presidency, Lyndon Johnson curtailed the practice of holding
White House conferences because so many had backfired on
him.

In summary, developments in television coverage have made
it possible for more demands to be articulated by groups within
the American political system, and the easiest focus is the
President. His resources for meeting new demands have not been
correspondingly enlarged. Therefore, public response adds a
new facet to the paradoxical nature of Presidential power. Yet
another facet is provided by the lack of power to effect the
new economic responsibilities that he has been given.

INCREASING ECONOMIC RESPONSIBILITIES

Because the typical American lacks a clearly patterned ideology
in policy areas and tends to vote on the basis of his group interest
or the nature of the times, it is possible for a high level of public
expectation of Presidential economic initiative to coexist with
a high level of public distrust of governmental interference.
With apparent ease, large numbers of Americans can respond
to any difficulty with the cry "there oughta be a law!" while
staunchly maintaining that "that government is best which
governs least." The President is often trapped between these
two bits of folk wisdom.

Although Americans have passed a number of laws to involve
the President directly in economic planning, such as the Budget
and Accounting Act of 1921, the Employment Act of 1946, and
the Taft-Hartley Act of 1947, they have carefully avoided giving

him adequate means to achieve his plans. In practice, there is generally resistance to any major plan on his part. Moreover, the constitutional system of checks and balances provides adequate means to block any Presidential economic initiative that is not well supported. Therefore, the increasing economic responsibilities that contemporary Presidents must assume constitute some of the more frustrating aspects of office.

The President has been given two institutions to help him in economic planning, the Bureau of the Budget and the Council of Economic Advisers. While he can derive great benefit from them, there are obvious limitations on the degree to which they can be useful. The Council of Economic Advisers is particularly handicapped by the fact that the requirements of current economic theories are such that its advice is often likely to be of a nature on which he cannot effectively act.

Prescriptions for the Nation's Economic Health

Purposeful use of modern economic theory in the formation of public policy is a fairly recent practice in the United States. Until Franklin Roosevelt's day, the nation followed orthodox fiscal policy, which stressed the balanced budget. Once tax policy had been set, a government could estimate its income and determine what it would be able to spend. Little relation was seen between fiscal, tax, and monetary policy. Each existed in a separate compartment until the Great Depression made it necessary to reexamine the situation. It thus became necessary to face the basic problem arising from dependence on orthodox fiscal policy: the inevitable cycle of boom and bust, inflation and depression, which occurred while it was in use. One possible alternative to orthodox fiscal policy was presented by Lord Keynes.

John Maynard Keynes had proposed that money could have a "multiplier effect"—that each dollar released by the government could stimulate private economic transactions involving many times one dollar. This multiplier concept required a new attitude toward the government's role in the economy. It suggested that the best way to free a nation from economic depression was to forget about balanced budgets and concentrate instead on getting money to many individuals either by lowered taxes or by government spending for goods and services such as schools, dams, roads, and hospitals. Either way, the government would be putting money into circulation, which would have a multiplier effect. Naturally, there would be a governmental deficit, but the measures which created the deficit (lowered taxes and increased spending) would start an economic spiral. This would raise the national income so significantly that there would be a great deal more income to tax. Thus, it was expected that this surge of economic growth would eliminate the deficit created by the government's pump priming methods.

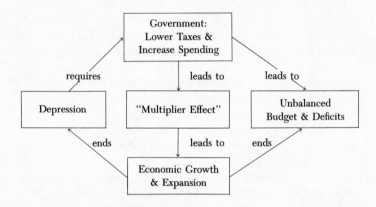

Keynes may have had an answer for the Great Depression, but getting Americans to use it was another story. They had just elected a pragmatist to deal with the Great Depression, and Roosevelt was buying no broad, overarching theories or crusades. He was simply trying to deal with the problem posed by unprecedented unemployment and failing banks. The President fully believed in the truth of orthodox fiscal policy but felt that emergency measures had to be taken in this instance. Because people had to be put to work, he embarked on a vast policy of federal spending, which provided jobs and wages. Naturally, this caused a large budget deficit, but the economy started to recover. Thus, his *ad hoc* method of dealing with the crisis followed the Keynesian script. A happy ending seemed assured, but this did not last long. As Americans began to recover from the Depression there seemed no need to maintain emergency measures. Roosevelt returned to a balanced budget by reducing government spending. At the same time the Federal Reserve tightened the flow of money. The result of these two changes was a severe slump in 1938. The full implications of Keynes' theories had yet to be faced and accepted.

Nevertheless, one change in the nature of Presidential economic responsibilities had gained widespread acceptance. In his State of the Union message and other messages, Franklin Roosevelt placed before Congress a regular assessment of the nation's economy. The public expectation which twenty years of that practice had reinforced was embodied in the Employment Act of 1946. It required every President to maintain a general watchfulness over the state of the nation's economy, constantly diagnosing the nation's economic ills, and prescribing for them at least annually. A Council of Economic Advisers, composed of three professional economists, was created by the Act as a belated recognition that the President would need specialized assistance to deal with the responsibilities that were acknowledged as his routine obligation. Under President Truman the Council functioned as a mechanism for reviewing the economic health of the nation and proposing policies to deal with crises. It was less active under President Eisenhower. President Kennedy launched it on a course, which has been continued by President Johnson, of general review of economic policy and active planning.

The difficulties faced by the President and his Council of Economic Advisers are caused by changing American attitudes toward economic policy. There are three aspects of economic policy, only one of which can be considered the primary responsibility of the Council. Monetary policy, or policy concerning the quantity of money in circulation and the interest rate, is primarily the responsibility of the Federal Reserve Board. The Board may take independent action as it did in January, 1966, by raising the interest rate, despite Presidential objection. In tax policy the President has the initiative, but Congress has considerable authority and effectiveness and a very decisive veto, especially in the House Ways and Means Committee. The only area of economic policy in which the President (and therefore his Council of Economic Advisers) is relatively free is in the area of fiscal policy—the way money will be used during the fiscal year. The difficulty for the President and his Council is that as economic planning has developed, fiscal policy has become increasingly involved with questions of monetary and tax policy. Keynesian economics assumed coordination of the three. As post-Keynesian thought developed to meet the problems inherent in Keynesian theories, coordination became even more important.

By Eisenhower's Presidency the problems of Keynesian thought were becoming more evident. One of these was an apparent assumption that budget deficits were an automatic cure for recession. President Eisenhower was fairly orthodox in his fiscal proposals, focusing on a balanced budget, though he only managed to attain it twice in eight years. When his attempt to balance the budget promoted recession in 1958, he was unwilling to pump money into the economy to get things going, which would have created a deliberate deficit. Because he failed to do this, the economy continued to drop so that the tax revenues fell off sharply. Eisenhower was left with both a recession and the largest budget deficit in the postwar period.

Another problem posed by Keynesian prescriptions in the American setting is that they deal more effectively with recession than inflation. Keynes' theory had a simple answer for inflation—do the opposite of what is necessary to recover from recession, *i.e.*, raise taxes and lower government spending. There should then occur a general cooling off of the overheated economic machinery.

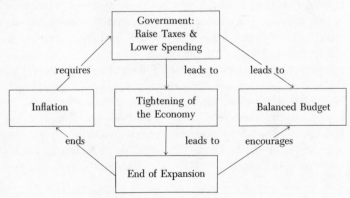

Theoretically, this should be no more difficult to accomplish than the steps for dealing with recession, but in practice it is *extremely* difficult. The politics of depression cannot easily be turned upside down to deal with inflation. In a recession the Council of Economic Advisers can propose a tax cut. Because Congress is involved in taxing policy, tax cuts will never occur at the time and in the way that the Council advises, but as there is much political mileage in cutting taxes, Congress is likely to act in some measure along the guidelines the Council has set. However, in a period of inflation the Council will propose a tax increase which is so politically objectionable, especially during an election year (every other year for members of the House of Representatives), that it is unlikely that the tax increase will occur at all. Certainly, it will not occur at the time when it is most needed. The *best* that can be expected is long delay, as President Johnson discovered with his request for a surcharge tax late in 1966. Because he knew that he could not succeed, he did not even propose a tax increase at the time when his advisers told him that it would be most useful, in mid-1966, before the Congressional elections. Even after the elections it was continually delayed, finally taking effect in the fall of 1968. It appears that Congressmen will only accept Keynesian prescriptions for recession, not inflation. Consequently, the political system is likely to be prey to continued periods of inflation during which the President will be expected to act at the same time that his proposals will be ignored—not a happy prospect for the contemporary President.

Another difficulty posed by Keynesian thought was its emphasis on quantity spending. It gave little thought to the fact that getting money into many hands indiscriminately might have no relation to the multiplier effect, as not all people will spend their entire increase on goods and services. Money tucked in the sugar bowl or mattress hardly aids a depressed economy. Most important of all, Keynesian thought was unable to deal with the fact that different types of spending lead to different rates of productivity.

In an attempt to deal with some of the discrepancies produced by Keynesian theory, a post-Keynesian theory developed. Its basic concept was that the relation between deficits and inflation was not simple, but that government expenditures or tax programs must be carefully tailored. Economic recovery was not considered a question of wholesale pumping of dollars into the economy. Rather, it seemed necessary to direct those dollars to areas that would stimulate the greatest economic activity and would have the highest social payoff. It was therefore thought necessary to cut taxes for those groups that would use the money for economic expansion. A basic assumption was made in post-Keynesian economics that as the economy grew it would reach a level at which the tax structure would become a drag on further expansion. This would occur because, as the economy grew, a graduated tax schedule would take an increasingly large part of the increases, reducing the money available for expansion. As the tax level went up, the returns on investment would decline and investment would decrease. Therefore, growth would decrease. (This was characterized as "fiscal drag.") The answer provided by post-Keynesian economics was *periodic tax cuts*, tailored for those areas where the tax structure had become a drag on expansion. The tax cut would free money for expansion, which would cause economic growth. As the economy grew, there would be more to tax, so the lower rate would not decrease revenue. In short, post-Keynesian economics maintained that government revenues could be created by cutting taxes if the *right type* of taxes were cut. It also suggested the need for selective tax adjustment in which incentives were given to manufacturers for expansion in the form of tax credit for investment.

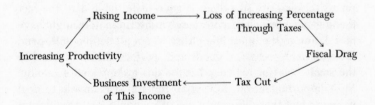

President Kennedy appointed Walter Heller, a major spokesman for this theory, as chairman of the Council of Economic Advisers. He continued in the post under President Johnson. His difficulties in that role suggest the limitations on the Council of Economic Advisers as aides for the President. President Kennedy was faced with a recession, for which the Council advised a tax cut. Congress resisted throughout Kennedy's lifetime, and only passed a badly mangled version of his proposal after his assassination. The Johnson administration was reluctant to propose appropriate measures to deal with inflation because of the political risks involved.

As long as the Council of Economic Advisers continues to formulate fiscal policy in terms of tax policy, it will involve the President in a struggle with Congress from which he is unlikely to emerge victorious, especially in dealing with inflation. A means to attain a similar end with greater potential success for the President would be formulation of fiscal policy on the basis of government spending rather than taxation. Spending is easier to cut than taxes and is more subject to Presidential control, but even this will be difficult. Congressional districts and interest groups develop a vested interest in governmental spending. It may be *easier* to cut government spending than to raise taxes during an inflation—but it will never be easy. Furthermore, the wrong types may be cut to protect the pork barrels of influential Congressmen. Federal spending on the poverty program is more likely to be cut in an economy move than non-essential defense contracts with manufacturers in the districts of influential Congressmen.

Thus, the Council of Economic Advisers is a body whose prescriptions are necessary for the President to fulfill his obligations under the Employment Act. However, as their prescriptions are currently based on post-Keynesian economics, which involves fiscal policy with tax policy, they commit the President to a heavy expenditure of prestige and time in a venture that has marginal chances of success, especially when inflation is involved. This deserves particular attention in view of the fact that the general economic prospect for the politically significant future is inflation.

For the prescriptions of post-Keynesian economics to be effective, fiscal policy must also be coordinated with monetary policy, yet the President has no way to compel coordination of the two. Monetary policy is the responsibility of the Federal

Reserve Board. As has been noted, the Board is capable of independent action. The United States is the only industrial economy that has this division. The lack of coordination weakens America's ability to act quickly and weakens the effectiveness of both its fiscal and monetary policy.

Moreover, it should not be forgotten in this focus on public economic policy that the United States has a mixed economic system in which many of the most important sectors of the economy are in private hands. In such a system it is impossible to ensure compliance with public economic policy. It is necessary to provide inducements to get the private sector to comply with the public one. For example, the President may set wage-price increase guidelines on the basis of recommendations by the Council of Economic Advisers, but he cannot force industry or labor to comply with them. To carry out his economic responsibilities, the President must be skillful at persuading more than Congress. The most dramatic recent confrontation of a President with one element of the private economic sector was Kennedy's disagreement with Roger Blough over a price rise in the steel industry which exceeded the Council's wage-price guidelines. Even here, a case study of the incident has demonstrated that good fortune and the power of the market, not Presidential power, were responsible for Kennedy's success:

> ... President Kennedy gave a virtuoso performance of simulating action and the situation was successfully disguised. Perhaps his greatest achievement lay in holding the diverse elements of his administration together and creating a facade of unity in government. This required intense effort and much skill, but it could not have continued for long. Events rescued the President. Nevertheless, the administration's venture came perilously close to an exposure of impotence.[22]

The influence the Council of Economic Advisers will have on governmental policy and its usefulness to the President depend heavily on the personality of the chairman and his conception of the Council's role.[23] His vigor helps to shape the institution. If he has the patience and capacity to transmit complicated economic theories to Congress in a manner that enables it to see where action must lie, there is greater likelihood that Council prescriptions will be followed. Truman's first chairman, Edwin G. Nourse, was not interested in educating

Congress, and therefore it showed little interest in his prescriptions. The second chairman, Leon Keyserling, conceived his role as that of an educator and therefore had a far greater impact on public opinion and Congress. Eisenhower's two chairmen, Arthur F. Burns and Raymond J. Saulnier, had a passive relationship with Congress. They would provide all the information Congress requested but volunteered little of their own. Walter Heller, who was chairman under Presidents Kennedy and Johnson, could only be described as an economic evangelist with a great deal of political sensitivity. He tailored economic information carefully to the self-interests of Congressmen. In proposing a tax cut, for example, he presented a chart by which each Congressman could see at a glance how his constituency would benefit with both minimum and maximum estimates. President Johnson's appointee, Gardner Ackley, had more trouble communicating, although he still believed in the educational function. He was assisted, however, by the impact of the work of his predecessors, Keyserling and Heller. Congress was far more sophisticated because of the lessons it had received, and many sections of the attentive public were more able to make intelligent decisions on economic policies because of the educational work the Council had engaged in. In ten years the Council of Economic Advisers had evolved as one of the more important institutions assisting the President, thanks largely to its chairmen.

Although its recommendations may be politically difficult, there are several ways in which the Council can be an asset to the President. Its primary asset is that of a highly mobilized technical tool to formulate economic policies and gain support for them. It can provide valuable professional ammunition in support of his economic policy. As Walter Heller wrote, it should and can "fit his philosophy and further his high purpose."[24] Above all, it is useful because it is specific. It can provide a clearly formulated set of measures to back up party platform pledges. It can be used, as in Kennedy's disagreement with Roger Blough, to provide facts and figures on short notice to support the President's position.[25]

Finally, the requirements of post-Keynesian economics can be partially met without tax, monetary, and private economic coordination. Fiscal policy implies the speed of spending, and this can be controlled through the Bureau of the Budget. When Eisenhower was faced with the recession of 1958 he pushed the interstate highway program, and the building of a number of new post offices for which money had already been appropriated. The President also has certain discretionary controls on the economy, for example, letting of contracts, hiring, and firing. These also affect the flow of funds.

Nevertheless, the dependence of post-Keynesian economics on a coordination of fiscal, tax, and monetary policy, which also requires cooperation from the private sector of the economy, forces the President to rely on moral suasion as his ultimate authority. This is one example of the Presidential paradox of economic responsibility with inadequate power.

Involvement in Labor Disputes
Another example of the President's responsibility and impotence is given by his routine involvement in major labor disputes. The idea that he must be routinely involved in labor disputes of national significance stemmed from the interventions of Grover Cleveland in the Pullman strike and Theodore Roosevelt in the coal strike. Both men felt the pressure of public expectation that a President must act to end a threatened national emergency, whether he had *de jure* power or not. Eventually, this expectation was put into statutory form in the Taft-Hartley Act of 1947. It prescribed that the President must establish a fact-finding board to make a report on the dispute, order the Attorney General to issue an eighty-day injunction against a strike call if that seemed best, authorize a vote on management's last offer, and if the dispute continued beyond the eighty-day cooling-off period, he must make recommendations to Congress.

In effect, the statute is a quiet source of blackmail against the President. In labor disputes he is expected to accomplish an accord which prevents the economy from being disrupted by a strike in a major industry. He is given responsibility for protecting the public with no means to enforce compliance with his suggestions. As has been suggested, the process of election makes any President most sensitive to states with large blocs of Electoral College votes, *i.e.*, urban, industrialized states. Therefore, Presidents of both parties must consider and be responsive to the labor vote. Consequently, it is usually inexpedient for any President openly to champion management's cause in a labor dispute. Thus it is management which must be convinced to make the requisite concessions, but the President has no guaranteed leverage against it. If he fails, public expectations are disappointed, and his loss of prestige may jeopardize his chances to effect important parts of his program. If, on the other hand, he is successful, his increased public prestige can be a persuasive lever on Congressmen to assist him in attaining other goals. He is trapped by the need to succeed to avoid jeopardizing his program, and the end result is usually that the President is forced to make concessions to management such as tax rebates or dropping anti-trust suits pending in the Department of Justice in return for their settlement with labor. Management suffers no loss because the expense (plus an extra charge, as a rule) is merely passed on to the consumer in the form of price increases. Typically, headlines will proclaim the President successful in ending the threatened strike. Then a day or so later there will be a small article reporting some advantage accruing to management from the federal government. For example, after President Johnson's well publicized settlement of the impending railway strike in the spring of 1964, articles appeared about his pressure on the House Rules Committee to dislodge a bill granting the railroad industry greater freedom to set rates and his pressure on the Internal Revenue Service to allow depreciation for bridge and tunnel construction.[26] Presidential success in applying the Taft-Hartley Act has a high price tag and is definitely not guaranteed.

Coordinating the Executive Budget
The growing public expectation that the President would coordinate executive spending led to passage of the Budget and Accounting Act of 1921. Perhaps, because his responsibilities under this Act have a less immediate impact on the general public, it would appear to be the least difficult among his increased economic responsibilities.

Prior to this Act each government department submitted estimates for the coming fiscal year to the Treasury Department. Treasury merely compiled them and transmitted them to eight relevant standing committees in each House. Occasionally, Presidents would make sporadic interventions, but they lacked statutory or customary authority to force changes in departmental budgets and therefore had to bargain with the department representatives. Theodore Roosevelt took the initiative and called a Cabinet meeting to discuss estimates in an attempt to bring some coordination into the process. After a long period of agitation for reform this administrative innovation was enacted into law.

The Budget and Accounting Act had three major provisions. Congressional committees dealing with the budget were reduced from eight to one in each house, the Appropriations Committee. The estimates that they received were to come from the President as an Executive Budget. No department was authorized to transmit estimates to Congress. In order to assist the President in formulating the budget, a Bureau of the Budget was established in the Treasury Department. Following recommendations of the 1937 Brownlow Report, it was transferred to the White House Office and underwent a thoroughgoing reorganization. During Truman's administration it became more than a budget agency, as the assistant to the President, John R. Steelman, used it to handle "family fights" in the executive branch.[27] It also provided an important recruiting ground for White House Staff. In Eisenhower's hierarchy the Bureau of the Budget was responsible to Sherman Adams. Kennedy used it more actively than had Truman, and Johnson continued this practice.

Formally, the Bureau of the Budget's purpose is to engage in the year-long budget process which covers the fiscal year from July 1st to June 30th. Every department must develop its own estimates of necessary budget items for the coming year, which it submits to the Bureau of the Budget. The Bureau holds hearings on these estimates, organizes the overall budget proposal in line with the President's priorities and requirements, and submits it to him. Then the Bureau assists him in formulating the final form of the Executive Budget, which is presented to the House and Senate Appropriations Committees. The Bureau holds hearings, reformulates the budget, and engages in the long process of debate and negotiation prior to passage of the budget in its final version. Meanwhile, it is assisting the President to write and submit bills for supplementary appropriations, which will be presented through the year. Finally, the Bureau administers the details of appropriations bills once they have been passed.

Actually, the Bureau of the Budget is a Presidential resource far beyond its function in the funding process. During this process, the Bureau provides the President with two invaluable means of assistance: it gathers intelligence on the activities of the vast bureaucracy for which he is responsible, and it acts as a control mechanism on the bureaucracy.

The Bureau is in continuous contact with every department, bureau, and agency in the executive branch because of its responsibility for budget preparation, administration of the budget, and elements of organization and management. Therefore, it is a key source of information for the President on a wide spectrum of activity. As one recent study found, "When the President wants to know what is happening with respect to almost anything in some part of the Executive Branch he is likely to turn first to the Bureau of the Budget to report information to him."[28]

The Bureau has several means at its disposal to bring the bureaucracy into line with the President's priorities, including its functions in legislative clearance, impounding, and distributing funds unevenly. The capacity for legislative clearance is particularly important as a control mechanism, affecting the substance of departmental policy. As a part of the process of formulating the budget, it is necessary for departments to submit any bills they wish to have proposed to the Bureau. The Bureau will judge these proposals on the basis of the degree to which they fit into the President's budgetary and programmatic priorities. No legislation is likely to be proposed in the President's State of the Union message or in his special messages to Congress which has not been first cleared through the Bureau of the Budget. In this way the Bureau helps to monitor departmental activities.[29]

If the President wishes to prevent money that Congress has appropriated for a specific purpose from being spent, he can have the Bureau impound it. In this way the agency is never given the money and cannot engage in the activity to which the President objects. Such an action carries serious political risks, however, as Congress does not like to have its budgetary intentions trifled with. It can retaliate by eliminating appropriations for key sections of the President's program the following year. Impounding is thus a last resort and has been successful primarily on military appropriations where the President's prestige as Commander-in-Chief carries great weight. Impounding appropriations for farmers or veterans might be political suicide. This is one aspect of the dichotomy the President experiences between great limitation on his freedom of action in domestic affairs and the wide leeway given him in foreign affairs and defense.

The Bureau's ability to dispense funds unevenly provides a more subtle way of accomplishing the President's purpose. After Congress votes for appropriations, the Bureau normally allots them in quarterly installments. The manner in which it chooses to exercise this function (under the President's direction) will obviously affect policy areas. It may dispense the bulk of an appropriation in the first quarter if it is the President's judgment that Congress has been unnecessarily restrictive and will later be willing to vote a supplemental appropriation if the agency's funds are gone. (This technique has been used with notable success on foreign aid appropriations, allowing Congressmen to demonstrate economy on the widely publicized initial budget and acquiescence on its more obscure supplement.) On the other hand, if the President wishes to reduce a program that Congress has pressed upon him, yet dares not take the step of impounding, he may find it expedient to have the Bureau dispense minimal funds during the first three quarters. An agency would thus be unable to spend the remainder during the last quarter. Congressmen are aware of the significance of this maneuver, however, and can press the President before the second quarter to loosen the purse strings for their pet projects.

Clearly, there are a great many people who are highly motivated to work amicably with the Bureau of the Budget. Those agencies or departments that have little support outside of the executive branch are heavily dependent on the Bureau, because it represents a Presidential commitment. Even those agencies and departments that have resources elsewhere prefer to work through it as the Bureau can make independent action difficult.[30]

The Bureau can also assist the President in dealing with Congress. Many Congressmen are heavily dependent on the information given to them by the Bureau of the Budget in understanding and evaluating each annual budget. They have limited time and knowledge to devote to the convolutions of an extraordinarily complex document whose summary alone constitutes one volume.

In many ways, the Bureau of the Budget is a great institutional source of strength at the President's disposal. More than any other agency it has a strong allegiance to him.[31] Its personnel view themselves as a governmental elite and are not easily intimidated by other departments, agencies, interest groups, or Congressional committees. Their line of responsibility is clear to them. They are responsive to his criteria and his programs. The top man is appointed at the discretion of the President without Senatorial confirmation. Others are civil servants but act as his men. They are an excellent source of information because they know the President's priorities, can monitor departmental activities, suggest departmental change on points where conflict occurs with his priorities, and alert him if conflict persists. They are also a valuable source of expertise. They know the overall system, and any responsible official pays attention to what they say. Like his Staff, they also act as buffers for him, saying "no" for a lot of things and taking the heat from him.

Nevertheless, effective though it may be, there are limitations upon the degree to which the Bureau of the Budget can maintain Presidential control of his executive branch. As one writer noted, "The most serious obstacle to acceptance of Budget Bureau leadership is that Congress determines appropriations.... Hence the Bureau frequently accepts consistent Congressional action as a guide."[32] In short, the Bureau is unable to guarantee that an agency will receive the amount it has recommended because Congress can raise its estimates, or lower them. Therefore, the agencies make "end-runs" around the Bureau to gain Congressional support. The Bureau customarily responds by attempting to set its estimates in line with consistent Congressional action, in order not to lose face. Thus, if it is known that Congress customarily makes generous appropriations for an item such as Naval armaments, the Bureau will advise the President to do so too. In this way, agencies have become aware that if a choice must be made, their relations with Congress are more important than their relations with the Bureau, because consistent Congressional action will affect Bureau action.

Even after considering Congressional preferences, the Bureau cannot assure passage of the President's budget. Congress may cut his favorite programs, reorganize the priorities, and add new programs that he opposes. A recent example of the veto power that Congress can exercise over Presidential budgets was given in 1968. President Johnson had previously requested a ten per cent surcharge to the income tax, which was considered necessary to relieve inflation. Such a request had to be passed through the House Ways and Means Committee before it could be voted upon by House membership. This Committee's chairman, Wilbur D. Mills, was a conservative Democratic representative of about a half a million people in Arkansas, whose keynote had always been economy. Mills consistently refused to clear the surcharge unless the administration made extraordinary cuts in federal spending. Because the surcharge was essential to the President, his budget message of January, 1968, attempted to appease Mills by a monumental cut in domestic spending. This case demonstrates the vulnerability of Presidential budget requests to the pressures of individual Congressmen or groups of legislators. As one observer noted, "The interesting thing is how he [Mills] has been able to stymie the combined advocacy of the Administration, the Federal Reserve, most of the business community, and a sizeable proportion of the academic economists." [33] He could do this because of his expertise and leadership in the Committee, and his broader influence through the particular favors he could do for other Congressmen in terms of writing tax loopholes which they desired into revenue bills. [34]

In brief, the effect of all of the increased economic responsibilities which the President has received is to make management and manipulation of the economy a major preoccupation. This has become part of a triumvirate of concerns including foreign relations and military affairs which are the primary and constant focus of the Presidency. However, unlike foreign relations and military affairs, the President's economic responsibilities far outstrip the means at his disposal to achieve success. As one writer has commented, "The Presidency has gradually acquired far more responsibility for prosperity—in the eyes of business, labor and voters—than it has authority to act to promote or preserve it." [35]

CHANGING RELATIONSHIP WITH CONGRESS AND HIS PARTY

To a significant degree each of the changes which have been discussed change the relationship between Congress and the President. For example, the regular economic prescriptions that are expected of him, or his capacity to dominate the media, thereby overshadowing other public figures, affect the legislative branch as well as the executive. One expectation which has become routinized deserves particular notice because of its more direct impact on their relationship—the annual legislative program.

Annual Legislative Program

Since Truman's Presidency, the President has been expected to present an annual legislative agenda in every area of legislative action and to send bill drafts to Congress under his *own* name. Therefore, after his annual State of the Union message, he must present a budget message and economic report, followed by special messages and draft bills on every major area of legislation he desires. Congress expects this as a routine service and expressed its disapproval in strong terms when President Eisenhower did not provide the agenda in 1953. He had considered it a Democratic usurpation of Congress' prerogative, but his Republican legislature disagreed. Thereafter, he presented an annual legislative program, as did his successors.

The program was considered valuable by Congress because it gave advance information on Presidential priorities, provided an immediate work load for every legislative committee, and increased the publicity value for Congressmen in either sponsorship of or opposition to the President's bills. Therefore, it was described by one critic as a service function which in no way obligated Congress.[36] Such a description emphasizes the problems of Presidential "clerkship" by maintaining that no President can get everything he wants, and that the measures which are passed do not necessarily appear in the form requested. At the same time, his prestige is on the line and is consequently bound to suffer. This would seem to overstate the President's weakness and underestimate the value of the program to him.

From the President's perspective, the asset of providing an annual legislative agenda lies in the fact that public debate will be concerned largely with the issues with which he is concerned. Because he will have initiated that debate, it will occur on his terms. He can arrange to present his ideas in their most favorable light, taking full advantage of his unique capacity to gain publicity and public attention in order to inform and influence the ensuing debate.

The custom has fundamentally altered the relationship between Congress and the President in the sense that most of Congress' agenda now comes from a source external to the legislature. Through the annual legislative program the President shares the function of setting the Congressional agenda with the majority (and minority) leadership in each house. This provides him with a significant base of power. Naturally, the President is not assured passage of his program in exactly the form in which it is presented, but he has many assets and possible strategies to maximize his position. For example, he has sources of information in the press, his own executive branch, and in his party's leadership in the legislature which can indicate the type of opposition that is likely to form. Once he knows this, he can act accordingly. One possible strategy is to request more than he actually expects in order to have points on which to bargain while safeguarding his real priorities. He also has many useful tools to bargain with legislators, such as his ability to include programs they want in his program, supporting them for reelection, or threatening to veto measures of which he does not approve. Necessarily, there will be some compromises, but a skillful President can use the annual legislative program as more of an opportunity for influence than is indicated by those who stress his clerkship.

The need to deal with Congress on a continuous lobbying basis has caused Presidents to establish specialized staff. For example, during the War Franklin Roosevelt created the post of Special Counsel to the President for Judge Samuel Rosenman.

It formalized the functions he had been unofficially performing for several years: drafting speeches and messages to Congress and reviewing all bills and executive orders on the basis of legal and policy considerations. In his organization of the White House Staff, President Truman placed one Administrative Assistant, Charles Murphy, in charge of Congressional liaison work. Supporting staff were also developed. His successors have continued to enlarge the staff members responsible for legislative liaison work, helping to increase the President's direct and continuous overview on his program.

Partisan Responsibilities

The changes which have altered the President's relations with Congress have had a similar impact on his political party. Those changes, for example, which have resulted in public focus on the President and increasing public influence on the Presidential nomination process have correspondingly increased the possibilities for an incumbent President to dictate the choice of successor for his party's nomination. Paradoxically, this has increased the significance of the Vice-Presidency because the office is an excellent one in which to place a chosen successor.[37]

The President has a high degree of control over the choice of his running mate at a convention, and the office provides an excellent opportunity (if the President chooses to use it that way) for the occupant to receive favorable publicity and build his public image. If the Vice-President is considered weak on foreign affairs he can be given experience and publicity in this field by sending him on missions abroad, as, for example, Nixon's trips to Moscow and Latin America, or Johnson's trips to Latin America, Asia, Scandinavia, and Berlin. The Vice-President's position on the National Security Council and Cabinet can be well publicized. He can be used as a Presidential liaison with party, Congressional, state, or interest group leaders. Naturally, his leadership image will be enhanced if he must take over during Presidential illness (Nixon) or after the death of the President (Truman, Johnson).

The names of the President and Vice-President are almost the only ones in America which become household words except for victorious generals (a disappearing breed), astronauts (whose

impact diminishes as their number increases), and stars of television, motion pictures, and sports. Senators or Governors are
not usually as widely known. Representatives are often not even
known within their own constituencies. This is one of the reasons
that the contemporary path to the Presidency is generally barred
to the non-millionaire. In a large, heterogeneous, politically
apathetic nation with a decentralized party system, it takes a
fortune for someone whose name is not widely known to be
able to attain the elective or appointive office *from which* to
launch a campaign for the Presidential nomination in terms of
publicity, travel, brain trusts, speech writers, and all the panoply
necessary to capture public attention and be perceived as of
Presidential stature. The Vice-Presidency has these resources (if
a President chooses to allow such a role to his Vice-President),
which makes it almost the only position from which a man
lacking access to millions may hope to attain the Presidency,
e.g., Truman, Nixon, and Humphrey.

From Van Buren to Eisenhower, no Vice-President was
nominated as his party's candidate for the Presidency unless he
had already become President through the death of the incumbent. Candidates came from the Senate, Cabinet, or Gov-
ernorships. Since then, there have been three Vice-Presidents,
each of whom has been considered a significant contender for the
office of President. Eisenhower chose Nixon to follow him.
Kennedy's assassination interfered with that process, but he was
quoted as saying that if he were not President he knew of no one
better qualified for the job than Lyndon Johnson.[38] Johnson made
similar statements with regard to Humphrey. The election of
1968 underscored this trend, as the incumbent Vice-President
campaigned against a former one. Nixon's choice of Spiro T.
Agnew was a notable exception to the trend.

Maintaining influence over the choice of a successor has been
made imperative, and in some cases much easier, by passage
of the Twenty-Fifth Amendment in 1967. That Amendment
ended all previous constitutional doubt that a Vice-President
could serve as Acting President during Presidential illness. It
insured Presidential control over choice of his Vice-President
in some instances by providing that on the death of a Vice-
President the President would nominate a successor, and that

when a Vice-President became President through death of the incumbent, he would nominate a new Vice-President. While controlling the choice of a successor to take charge of the party is not a substitute for being personally in command, it is a very useful device in maximizing personal control within the party.

A second example of routinized partisan obligations has a similar effect upon the President. The practice of campaigning for the return of members of his party in Congress during an off-year election is not an assurance of partisan support for his legislative programs. Yet, if he is successful, it does create a series of obligations that can be helpful.

The problems attendant upon such a role were clearly demonstrated by Woodrow Wilson and Franklin Roosevelt. Wilson caused a furor in 1918 when he campaigned for the return of legislators who would support his policies on the League of Nations. Roosevelt's ill-conceived 1938 campaign intended to purge his own party of Congressmen who disagreed with him. Both men demonstrated the fact that decentralized parties limit the capacity of any President to gain a legislature of his choosing. His nation-wide popularity is irrelevant for this purpose. In order to have an effect on a legislator's career, he must have leverage on that man's constituency. If it is a one-party area, without competition in the party primaries, such leverage is highly unlikely. It is also improbable where the constituency disagrees with the President's program, as do many Southern districts on civil rights. However, where the President is popular and the constituency is competitive he is likely to be able to have some impact. His aid is therefore likely to be sought by his party's Congressional candidate in that district. The degree to which his party has come to expect him to provide that service was demonstrated by Republican reaction to President Eisenhower. He considered such activity to be a Democratic innovation, which he did not intend to continue. Instead of applauding his respect for the separation of the branches, Congressional Republicans turned so wrathfully on their Chief that he was forced reluctantly into the role. Although it is clearly a service that Presidents are expected to provide, it is also one from which they are likely to benefit. If the President is popular in the district and the candidate for whom he campaigns wins,

Presidency and the party system are mutually interdependent support for his legislative measures, because a President who has leverage in a legislator's constituency may not be lightly ignored.[39]

Presidents have recognized their need for continuous help with partisan matters by appointing White House Staff for the purpose. For example, Franklin Roosevelt created the post of Special Executive Assistant to the President for Eugene Casey to serve as special coordinator on party matters. Under Truman one Administrative Assistant, Donald Dawson, coordinated matters of personnel and patronage, with the aid of his own staff. Sherman Adams handled these questions as the Assistant to the President under Eisenhower. Succeeding Presidents also had staff men assigned primarily to partisan matters, Kenneth O'Donnell for President Kennedy and Marvin Watson for President Johnson. They gathered information, and acted as his representatives and as buffers for him.

INCREASING FOREIGN AND DEFENSE RESPONSIBILITIES

Either through statute or custom, a number of new responses have come to be routinely expected of the President in the field of foreign relations and defense, further necessitating growth of institutionalized assistance. These responsibilities include summit meetings and ceremonial visiting, coordinating the nation's defense measures even in peacetime, and a new involvement with science and technology.

Summit Meetings and Ceremonial Visiting

Summit meetings and ceremonial visiting have become routinely expected of Presidents primarily since the 1950's. A summit conference is a meeting of the President with other chiefs of state. Although the term had not been coined in Woodrow Wilson's day, he was the first President to go abroad for such a meeting to sign the Versailles Treaty after World War I. At the time grave doubts were expressed about the constitutionality of having a President leave the country. The press and Congressmen questioned the wisdom of Wilson's act on several grounds. Because Atlantic crossings took considerable time in those days and communication was less certain, they complained that the President would be unable to keep up with his work. Today that criticism has less relevance, although a man engaged in an international tour must certainly devote a great deal of his limited time and energy to it and make it the focus of attention for key staff members and advisers.

Two other criticisms, however, have increasing relevance. There was fear for the President's personal safety from accident or assassination attempt, and that problem has hardly diminished. Assassination is not a peculiarly American aberration, and its repercussions are heightened in a nuclear age.

A second, and related, criticism concerns the physical strain of such conferences for the President. International travel has magnified this problem. Wilson lived in an age of leisurely travel, entertainment, and negotiation. Jet age travel catapults a President and his advisers across time zones with a speed that scientists have proved upsetting to "biological clocks," and therefore especially tiring. He is expected to hop off the plane into a whirl of activity, both diplomatic and social, which covers every waking hour. He will probably visit several capitals in transit and return to his desk within less time than it took Wilson to cross the Atlantic. Because communication has improved, he will have to do all this while he continues to be under the pressure of dealing with events at home.

Given these drawbacks, no President until Eisenhower considered summit conferences as anything but an emergency measure connected with wartime. It was in this vein that Roosevelt met with allied heads of government during the Second World War, and Truman went to Potsdam. Eisenhower was the first President to travel abroad during peacetime when he went to Geneva in 1955 and Paris in 1960. He also became an enthusiastic traveler in his capacity as Chief of State. He developed the practice of minimizing formal meetings in preference to informal ones with single chiefs of government or *ad hoc* groups.

Since Eisenhower's Presidency, "summitry" and ceremonial visiting have been justified on the ground that they provide an opportunity to focus world attention on an important problem, to deal with that problem, to become personally acquainted with

other chiefs of state, and to win their respect. It also brings a
great deal of prestige if the problem is dealt with successfully.
Each of these justifications rests on shaky premises if examined
closely. Under conditions in which men communicate through
interpreters at brief sessions and are aware that they are being
assessed, their responses will be guarded. Moreover, American
Presidents will also be scrutinized and might demonstrate weaknesses that would harm further international communication.
It was no asset to America's relations with Russia that their
representatives learned at first hand how dependent President
Eisenhower was on the opinions and ideas of John Foster
Dulles.[40]

If prestige is a direct result of success, its converse is also
true, and success in summitry is no easy matter.[41] It is dangerous
for international leaders to confer without substantial accomplishment. Expectations raised by such a trip can seriously
backfire if they are disappointed, as Eisenhower learned when
the U-2 incident undermined his Paris meeting with Khrushchev.
Success depends on more than effective public relations. To
accomplish something substantial, summit conferences must
occur *after* sustained diplomatic effort, not before or during it.
It is rarely possible during the few days available to unravel
the tangled web of differences on any major international
question such as disarmament. A great deal of unspectacular
diplomatic drudgery and negotiation must occur at a lower level
to produce an agreement that national leaders can sign with
glory. If the ploughing, planting, and tending have not been
successful, there can be no harvest. Fearing public reaction to
thwarted hopes, the President feels pressured into putting the
best face possible on the situation and resorts to distorted
descriptions of nebulous hopes like "the spirit of Camp David."
When dealing with a country like Russia such a "spirit" is, as
the word implies, an insubstantial apparition.

If believed, the President is trapped because he has encouraged public enthusiasm for the summit conference as a tool
of international diplomacy. If not believed, his prestige sinks
further and he may face serious problems in accomplishing his
domestic programs. It would seem that this was what Clinton
Rossiter meant when he said that the President "wears all his

hats" at once. Success in one aspect of his work will help others, and vice versa. Any President faced with pressure to go to the summit must ask himself, "Is this trip really necessary?"

President Kennedy's answer was a resounding "no." He saw the liabilities and pledged during his campaign that he and his Secretary of State would stay at home, but he had overlooked the impact of routinization. During the Eisenhower years a body of expectation had developed that an American President would confer with foreign chiefs of state, especially with Khrushchev. Eventually, Kennedy went to Vienna and Paris. He may have impressed De Gaulle and Khrushchev as a tough able, statesman, while Jacqueline captured all hearts, but concrete accomplishments were less impressive. In these conferences the real significance of the summit became more clear. It provides two types of service. First, it is a form of symbolic reassurance for the American people that their President is doing all he can to ease world tensions. Second, foreign leaders need him for personal political advantage and therefore request visits. It aids many political leaders to be seen as having close ties with the American President. It aids others politically to be seen as taking a strong stand against his policies, which provides symbolic reassurance for *their* constituents. Either way, summitry and ceremonial visiting can be useful for them, but not necessarily for the President. With good planning and good fortune these trips can be political triumphs as were Kennedy's visits to Berlin and Ireland, but there is invariably the dual danger of raising false hopes or of creating embarrassment. There are subtle long-range costs involved in terms of public disillusionment.

An unusual set of circumstances enabled President Johnson to limit summitry: the necessity of stabilizing domestic power after the assassination, the election campaign, Khrushchev's deposition, De Gaulle's intransigence, and Johnson's increasing international unpopularity over the Vietnamese War. This was only a temporary deflection of expectations, however. The Glassboro Conference of 1967, which was thrown together on the spur of the moment, suggests how intense are the pressures for summitry and how ineffective the practice can be. These pressures partially explain why one month after his inauguration President Nixon embarked upon a European tour. Given the risks involved in a trip to the summit and the impossibility of substantial accomplishment without previous diplomatic work, summitry cannot be considered a substantial addition to Presidential power.

Coordinating Military Policy

A new dimension has been added to Presidential power through the legal recognition of his responsibility to coordinate military policy, even in peacetime, and personally to approve the use of atomic weapons. The former responsibility was acknowledged in the National Security Act of 1947, the latter in the Atomic Energy Act of 1946.

It is surprising to learn how long it took for the concept to develop that military policy should be coordinated. Even at the height of the First World War President Wilson made only sparing attempts at coordination. There was no peacetime concern about such coordination until the period prior to American entry into the Second World War (1939 to 1941) during which Roosevelt tried to assert some control despite grave criticism. However, the cold war made it necessary on a routine, continuous basis in peacetime. Therefore, in 1947 the National Security Act provided that the President should be responsible for coordinating foreign and domestic military policy and gave him the assistance of a statutory cabinet committee of advisers, the National Security Council. Its membership included the President, Vice-President, Secretaries of State and Defense, and the Director of Emergency Planning,[42] plus any others the President might desire. It was created with two main functions. First, it was to provide guidelines for national security policy. It was to balance foreign commitments against military potential, and the Joint Chiefs of Staff were given the responsibility of determining the contribution of each military department. Second, it was to direct the work of the Central Intelligence Agency, which was established to coordinate and sift military and other intelligence information and inform the President and National Security Council.

Under President Truman the National Security Council began to meet and function during the Korean War as the statute had envisioned. However, problems appeared almost immediately which limited its usefulness for a President. Therefore, by 1951 it had been reduced to a paper-preparing organization. President Eisenhower restored its weekly meeting and further elaborated its institutional structure by adding a Planning Board to prepare agenda and an Operations Coordinating Board, which held monthly, quarterly, and annual reviews, "including mountains of follow-up memoranda, to ensure that each department and agency carried out the approved policy."[43] It was in the area of national security and foreign policy that President Eisenhower had chosen to exert his greatest influence, and he chose the National Security Council as his major source of coordination. All of his national security and foreign policy decisions were both developed and announced at its meetings.[44]

President Kennedy found it a far less useful institution. He abolished the Operations Coordinating Board in his first month in office and relegated the Planning Board to an inferior position. After the Bay of Pigs debacle, he fully realized the degree to which he alone was responsible for defense decisions and the degree to which his experts on the National Security Council were fallible.[45] Therefore, he held meetings far less frequently than had President Eisenhower, except during crisis periods, although individual members were brought in to clarify issues and argue them before the President. The primary purpose for which he held full Council meetings was symbolic reassurance for the advisers and the public.[46] He assuaged his military advisers by getting the views of every responsible officer on record at a time of crisis and silenced external critics "who equated machinery with efficiency."[47] Instead of relying on the full Council he preferred to set up *ad hoc* task forces that were specifically formed to deal with particular problems.[48] This led him to form the Executive Committee of the National Security Council, upon which he placed greater reliance. It was instrumental, for example, in helping him to formulate his policy on the Cuban missile crisis[49] and his Vietnamese policy.[50] President Johnson generally followed Kennedy's practice with regard to the Council.

This growing Presidential reluctance to depend on it was the outgrowth of a number of problems inherent in the institution.

Its usefulness as a tool of policy guidance is limited unless it meets very frequently, but frequent meetings take precious time from the other functions that its members must perform. Moreover, even after the Council has established guidelines, the President is fully responsible for all decisions made. When his security advisers make a mistake, as in the Cuban invasion, he must take full responsibility. Another difficulty raised by the National Security Council is its extremely narrow view of what is entailed in national security. It thinks of national security almost exclusively in terms of military strength. It would be more useful to the President if it could take a broader view. Finally, it has repeatedly demonstrated that it does not adequately control the Central Intelligence Agency. Whereas the advice of individual members in their capacities as Secretary of Defense or State, or one of the Joint Chiefs of Staff, may be very helpful to the President, the institutional meeting is not and is therefore held infrequently.

Despite the limitations of the National Security Council, the new responsibilities for coordinating military policy that came with it can be an asset to the President. Because there is a great imbalance in the degree of checks and supervision to which the President is subject in questions of defense, as opposed to domestic questions, any increase in his responsibility as Commander-in-Chief is likely to provide a means for increased power. Supported by public opinion, and provided with sufficient tools to put Congress at a bargaining disadvantage in the area of defense, this recently acquired responsibility for coordinating foreign and domestic military policy can be used to his advantage in a number of ways, which will be discussed in Chapter IV.

A similar argument may be made for the effect of the Atomic Energy Act of 1946. Before atomic weapons, no President had to approve use of any particular weapon. As an act of personal initiative, with Congressional compliance, Franklin Roosevelt undertook to commit the United States to the development of atomic weapons. By personal initiative Harry Truman authorized the first use of the atomic bomb. These precedents formed the background for the Atomic Energy Act, which required the President personally to review and approve weapons programs of the Atomic Energy Commission and personally to approve the use of atomic weapons. This gives a dimension to the President's function as Commander-in-Chief that it never had in peacetime, providing a further means for erosion of Congressional power in matters of defense.

Science and Technology

Questions of weapons development were only part of the President's growing responsibilities in the area of scientific and technological development. A number of other recent factors have led the public to expect him to be routinely involved in making key decisions in this area, including public concern for the damage to America's international prestige after 1957 Soviet launching of Sputnik I, a growing emphasis on peaceful applications of science and technology, and the development of types of scientific research that required federal subsidy. Inevitably, these expectations led to the establishment of supporting institutions with their attendant assets and liabilities.

As a result of the Sputnik launching, the post of Special Assistant to the President for Science and Technology was created, and the President's Science Advisory Committee (PSAC) was reconstituted as an advisory unit on questions of defense and science. This citizen's committee of eighteen eminent scientists and engineers functioned through panels that concentrated on providing the President with information on recent developments affecting matters of national security. The public concern generated by Sputnik also led to new means of federal aid for higher education, thereby routinely involving the President in consideration of the types and areas of science and technology that should be subsidized. In 1959 the Federal Council for Science and Technology (FCST) was established as part of the Executive Office of the President to coordinate these growing concerns and integrate the views of the various agencies involved.

Presidential emphasis on the use of science and technology underwent a marked shift during the late 1950's and early 1960's from a heavily military concern to one increasingly involved with peaceful application of science. Efforts by President Eisenhower to limit the spread of nuclear weapons became a major concern of President Kennedy and his Science Adviser. President Kennedy was also concerned with the potential of science and technology to meet economic and social needs. Among the questions requiring expert advice were the adequacy of natural resources, development of new water supplies, educational methodology, how to combat air and water pollution, and reform of mass transportation and public health.

A further factor influencing Presidential involvement in questions of scientific and technological advance was the development of "big science." By the 1960's types of scientific research such as high-energy physics, space exploration, and radio astronomy had become too expensive for private initiative and were increasingly dependent on federal subsidy. Through his involvement in the budget process, the President was inevitably involved with the development of "big science." In 1962, as a response to his need for greater assistance, Congress approved Reorganization Plan No. 2, which established the Office of Science and Technology (OST) in the Executive Office of the President. It became the central force among other advisers and groups in the field. The complexity and range of issues with which it dealt was summarized as follows: "Operating with PSAC and FCST, OST serves as the hub of an intricate communication network that spans all classical divisions of science and engineering, links together 300 officials in some 42 executive departments and agencies, and involves participation of some 300 leading authorities as consultants." [51]

The Office of Science and Technology and related assisting institutions are in a similar position to the Council of Economic Advisers in terms of their capacity to aid the President. They provide the advantages of expertise and information, and can be used as a lobbying group with Congress, the bureaucracy, interest groups, or the public. However, they also involve the President in responsibilities that may be difficult for him to accomplish.

One difficulty posed by this recent Presidential involvement in questions of science and technology is the accelerating speed at which change occurs. Programs become obsolete in a few years, but it is often difficult to prune them, redeploy resources, and restructure the bureaucracy that had developed around them. Thus, the pace of innovation exceeds the institutional means of response.

A further problem is posed by the differences between science and technology. A more immediately visible benefit occurs from subsidizing technological development, but long-range progress is impossible without basic scientific research. The President must make difficult choices between the two on the best way to allocate his limited resources. Consequently, here as elsewhere, his changing responsibilities provide a mixing blessing.

ROUTINIZATION AND INSTITUTIONALIZATION

Clearly, the joint trends of routinization and institutionalization have proved a mixed blessing for the contemporary President. They limit his freedom by forcing him to provide services for others, absorbing his time and attention, and borrowing his prestige for activities that may help others without assisting him. Routinization proves frustrating because the President may be required by custom or statute to fulfill certain expectations, but he receives no guaranteed support for his actions. Thus, initiative has been routinized, although success has not. Nevertheless, those same routines and institutions can be an aid to any President who will use them skillfully. Routinization causes him to provide services on which others are dependent, and institutionalization provides vantage points that can be very useful to a politically sensitive President. The Bureau of the Budget, Council of Economic Advisers, National Security Council, Office of Science and Technology, or White House Staff provides information and tools that enhance his capacity to bargain with interest groups, the bureaucracy, Congress, and the military.

One example of the type of asset that institutionalized assistants can provide is given by the White House Staff. It can help the President in several ways. His staff can gather information for him, can be used on spot assignments, are available to probe a given agency or problem in depth, and may act as his representatives on various committees and meetings. They are also an asset in the more subtle function of bargaining with key officials in the bureaucracy who enjoy a degree of freedom from Presidential control, which will be considered more fully in Chapter

III. His staff enable him to supervise a great number of agencies, whereas the President could only intervene personally in a few. A staff man spreads the President's control by suggesting to an agency that the staff man will request Presidential intervention if the agency does not comply. This does not necessarily mean that the agency will change radically, but to cut the risk of intervention it is likely to modify its demands or actions to some degree. The White House Staff also serve as buffers for the President, absorbing as many complaints as possible and keeping people from him. He refers to them people to whom he wants to say "no." Any good executive must establish such a dichotomy: his staff carries the bad news, he carries the good. They release trial balloons, sound out proposals, and initiate negotiations with leaders—all in a way that does not commit the President. When pressures on him become too severe, he can make a token sacrifice by dropping an adviser who was implicated in the crisis.

Thus, despite the handicaps inherent in continued routinization and institutionalization, there are assets as well. The difficulties inherent in maximizing these assets and minimizing their risks are heightened by the increasing isolation of Presidential office. This mixture of risk with asset, clerkship with leadership, exposure with isolation forms part of the paradox of the contemporary Presidency.

Presidential Leadership and Direction

Because the increasingly technical nature of many of the services that a President must perform and the increasing demands upon his time and energy make reliance on a staff necessary, the President is not so much the source of initiation in policy formation as the pivot around which the initiating process turns. His acquiescence is the minimal *sine qua non*. Therefore, his capacity to attract able advisers is very important. But the most significant factor will not be the qualities that the staff can provide for him; rather, it is the qualities of leadership and direction that he supplies for his staff. As has been suggested, the difference in usefulness of institutions such as the Bureau of the Budget or the Council of Economic Advisers depends upon the skill and perceptions of the President. This point is illustrated by the variety of ways in which contemporary Presidents have organized and used their White House Staff.

Franklin Roosevelt's methods of selection and use emphasized a generalist role for his staff members. There were no specialists, and no hierarchy. Rather, staff members had to be able to accept any assignment, and in order to have different viewpoints, President Roosevelt frequently encouraged staff rivalry by giving men similar assignments. He initiated the assignments, checked upon their progress, and personally received the final report. It has been said that

> The most impressive characteristic of the Roosevelt White House Office is the extent to which Roosevelt himself dominated its every activity. The staff was in a very personal sense an extension of the President.[52]

Recurrent obligations on the President's schedule made it useful to orient secretaries toward press relations and appointments, although they could be used for other purposes as well. World War II made it necessary to have greater formal organization, such as the Special Counsel, a Special Executive Assistant to the President, or a Chief of Staff to the Commander-in-Chief. Yet generalists still played a role, such as Harry Hopkins, who lived in the President's personal quarters as Special Assistant to the President and was involved in most aspects of White House policy. Throughout Roosevelt's Presidency "outsiders" like Benjamin Cohen and Thomas Corcoran were "borrowed" from executive departments. Although the President's contacts with his staff and capacity for direct supervision were curtailed during the war, he still maintained enough control, flexibility, and contact so that there was no hierarchy in the Eisenhower sense.

In a number of ways Harry Truman reorganized the White House Staff. While he aimed at having generalists on his staff, there was more organization and more fixed assignments for staff men, who were given supporting staff. Policy formation centered around the offices of the Assistant to the President, John Steelman, and the Special Counsel to the President (Samuel Rosenman to 1945 and Clark Clifford from 1946 to 1950). Truman also placed far more reliance than had his predecessor on the Cabinet and the Bureau of the Budget. This staff growth and formalization was a result both of personal preferences on the part of the President and the mounting pressures created by routinization. The options for experimentation with staff which his predecessor had enjoyed had been permanently curtailed, but Truman's organization retained a degree of flexibility unknown to his successor.

Accustomed to the hierarchical "Chief of Staff" organization of the Army, desirous of protecting the President from as many burdens as possible, and extraordinarily anxious to avoid staff dissent, President Eisenhower fundamentally reshaped the White House Staff, developing the first really hierarchical structure. Although Sherman Adams was given the title of the Assistant to the President, the functions of that office went far beyond those which John Steelman had fulfilled.

> Adams was, in every sense of the term, a Chief of Staff. He was at the top of the clearly structured hierarchy of the Eisenhower White House Office staff and that was the way Eisenhower wanted it.[53]

The President's appointments secretary was made responsible to Adams, most of the Special Counsel's duties were pruned away, and staff men were given fixed assignments and made directly responsible to Adams rather than to the President. The staff motto was: "Nothing should go to the President's desk if it could be handled elsewhere, and, if it had to go to the President, it should be condensed to a one page memo."[54] These memos had to include recommendations and were not permitted to reach the President without an "O.K., S. A." affixed to them. In his memoirs Sherman Adams indicated the extent to which Eisenhower's advisers were instrumental in deciding what he should do and persuading him to do it.

> I found early in the game that Eisenhower expected anyone who proposed a speech to him to have the reasons for making it thoroughly thought out, a draft on paper and the trip phased into his calendar. . . . I and the rest of the staff learned that we had to have a finished draft in shape in the President's hands at least two weeks before it was to be delivered so that he could put it into his desk drawer and brood over it at his leisure.[55]

In effect, Sherman Adams was the most important man in the executive branch on domestic affairs. He controlled all access and information to the President. All domestic policy decisions and appointments had to be cleared through him. His was an almost unquestioned voice on partisan political matters, because President Eisenhower was temperamentally indisposed to deal with any matter such as patronage. Adams synthesized all relevant domestic questions each day and sent them to the President in a brief report with any necessary clippings from the newspaper. Secretary of State John Foster Dulles filled a similar role in foreign affairs.

Thus, the President's primary functions were to review the actions of his chiefs and to make the requisite decisions on the policy alternatives presented to him. This proved a serious handicap to the President. Only the most significant crises of the day could appear in a brief daily synthesis, and only a few alternative policy choices could be presented. He had no glimpse of the smoke of potential fires, which might be put out before a blaze. Rather, he had to attend only to what was forced upon him by the logic of events. As he read only clippings instead of newspapers he was further isolated. With the best wills in the world, Dulles and Adams were still merely human and subject to the distortions of perception and understanding that are the human lot. The President isolated himself from the ideas of others, which might have provided balance. He had freed time at the expense of information, which caused him a number of unnecessary political embarassments. One of the most poignant moments of the Eisenhower years came when the President spoke to a television audience in 1959, trying to support Sherman Adams against attacks on Adams' injudicious relations with the Boston industrialist, Bernard Goldfine. With deep feeling the President said, "I need him." The need, however, was not respected, and Adams was forced to resign under mounting public and Congressional pressure. It was a serious blow to the President's organization, but one which forced him to take a more direct role in domestic affairs. The death of John Foster Dulles in the following year ended "deputy Presidents." Once his buffers were removed, Eisenhower became a more effective administrator of his White House Staff.[56]

There was a secondary aspect of Eisenhower's White House organization, which lasted through his Presidency. This was the great emphasis on formal committee mechanisms. The Cabinet was given a secretariat, which wrote up reports of Cabinet meetings and then held briefing sessions at the undersecretary level, after which reports were written up and circulated. Interdepartmental committees monitored by Presidential staff were established to narrow controversy to a small residue of issues. They too wrote reports and held briefings. In short, a vast, elaborate mechanism developed for reviewing, slowing, and providing maximum commentary on interdepartmental controversy. It was hard to implement action on the kinds (and quantity) of paper produced. The result was minimal action, which was reminiscent of the purpose for which one Canadian wit claimed that his country used committees:

> The necessity for action was clear to everyone,
> But the view was very general that nothing could be done,
> And the Government courageously decided that the Crown
> Should appoint a score of gentlemen to track the trouble down—
> Which always takes a long, long time.[57]

President Kennedy immediately terminated much of this formal structure and formal paper procedures. The Sherman Adams role was abandoned with its title. Paper work and hierarchical organization were severely pruned. In its place he maintained a number of key staff members with a core of fixed assignments (e.g., Congressional relations, public relations, appointments) but they were kept flexible, and no one had primacy. President Kennedy was his own Chief of Staff. Only the President gave directions, and he would assign his assistants to matters as he saw fit. "Kennedy reached out for advice from sources that seemed appropriate to a given task, doubtless accepted suggestions, but remained the pivot of the process and made the final choices."[58] All aides were given a "barging-in" privilege, which made the President continuously accessible to them.[59] He thus used Roosevelt's operating methods with a staff the size of Truman's.[60]

President Kennedy restored the position of Special Counsel to its significance under his Democratic predecessors, naming Theodore Sorensen to the post. Sorensen functioned as the President's primary speech writer and adviser on domestic matters. The primary adviser on foreign relations was McGeorge

Bundy. To the normal functions of Appointments Secretary, Kenneth O'Donnell added general "political troubleshooter."

As part of the necessary stress on continuity, President Johnson initially kept most of Kennedy's staff. Eventually, as they departed, a serious difficulty of the Johnson Administration became apparent—attracting staff. Johnson had a tendency, greater than any President since Roosevelt, to need a staff that was "intensely personal and absolutely tuned to his own work habits and needs." [61] Yet those work habits and needs were such that even admirers preferred to avoid working for him.[62] Departure of the three key Johnson appointees, Walter Jenkins, Jack Valenti, and Bill Moyers, were serious blows to his White House organization. Staff vacancies often remained unfilled or were filled after a delay. He therefore had to find alternative sources of assistance, and in doing so he came to rely on working through executive departments rather than his staff. He depended heavily on Secretary of State, Dean Rusk, and Secretary of Defense, Robert McNamara. In fact, Secretary McNamara was used for a broad range of policy areas from defense and foreign policy to civil rights. He also turned to three Washington lawyers for advice, James Rowe, Abe Fortas, and Clark Clifford. In time, Fortas and Clifford were brought into government positions.

This overview of the manner in which recent Presidents have used the White House Staff indicates that while his staff is essential in assisting the President to fulfill his routine obligations, its usefulness will depend heavily upon his personal inclinations and skill as an administrator. His leadership cannot be judged in terms of the speeches or innovations that he *personally* creates, but in terms of

> . . . how well he directs and synthesizes the efforts of his staff, and infuses them with a sense and appearance of common purpose, which is clearly recognizable as *his* purpose. . . . [A]ny political leader must use staff in much the way a craftsman uses tools. So long as they do the job intended they will be retained and used, but when they are no longer appropriate to the task in hand they will be put aside. . . . [T]he more successfully this is accomplished, the less room there is for the criticism that alien words are being put into his mouth.[63]

Whether presented by those who would assist the President

or by those who would curtail his power, proposals for further institutionalization must be assessed in relation to the crucial nature of Presidential leadership and the obstacles already placed on that path.

Proposals for Further Institutionalization

One author whose proposals were designed to curtail Presidential power was Edward Corwin. His fear of the "personalized" Presidency is shared by many who would like to check or limit the President by rigidifying the areas from which he can seek advice. It underlay Corwin's widely read proposal that Congress should institutionalize its leadership in a Joint Legislative Council from which the President would have to select his Cabinet.[64] Naturally, such a proposal would be balm to wounded Senators who felt that their institution had been unwisely eclipsed by the contemporary Presidency. Therefore, this or similar proposals have received periodic consideration and publicity. They are never enacted, however, because they are essentially irrelevant and dangerous.

In a very real sense they are irrelevant because quite the opposite process than personalization of the Presidency has occurred over the past four decades, in the sense that the force of a President's preferences and personality have actually been *limited* by the growth of routinization and institutionalization. When Richard Neustadt wrote that "all Presidents must now be strong," he was indicating that personal performance in office can no longer be as variable as it once was. In a more primitive governmental situation the man may make the institution, but in a mature, institutionalized situation he is far less free. Thus, the very trends that Professor Corwin has deplored as a source of personalization actually have an opposite effect.

Furthermore, routinization and institutionalization have not developed because of Presidential usurpation or personalization as Edward Corwin would have it, but because those innovations fit the needs of the President's various constituencies (electoral, congressional, bureaucratic, party, press, interest group, or international). Perhaps the clearest example of the degree to which they were demanded of succeeding Presidents despite personal preferences occurred during the Presidency of Dwight

David Eisenhower. Most of the initial types of innovation which became routinely expected were actions by Democratic predecessors, which President Eisenhower fundamentally opposed. On entering office he was determined to return the Presidency to Republican principles, which stressed separation of the branches, primacy of the legislature, and limitation on government intervention in the economy. Moreover, Eisenhower's personal conception of the Presidential office stressed its Chief-of-State aspects, minimizing his partisan role. When he first became President he did not deliver an annual legislative program, he did not wish to campaign for party members at the mid-term election, and his economic policy opposed Presidential interference. Nevertheless, Congress demanded a program and got it every year after the first, his partisans demanded and received increasing electoral support, and he was forced to make prescriptions for dealing with the nation's economic difficulties. Performance of these initiatives was demanded because they filled the needs of others besides the President.

Eisenhower's experience indicates that routinization and institutionalization of the Presidency were not the result of the willfulness of Franklin Delano Roosevelt, but of factors inside and outside the political arena which have increased the significance of the Presidency as a source of initiation and caused public attention to focus there. Those factors have created the context within which the contemporary President must function. The significance of these trends will be more fully discussed in connection with Congress, but a few will be suggested here.

The widespread agreement by the majority of the American people on economic intervention which was reflected in such statutes as the Taft-Hartley Act and the Employment Act has brought the Presidential office into a position of greater initiative. War, cold war, America's emergence as a world leader, and the increased importance of foreign relations have emphasized areas of initiative which were always the President's. Population and the number of federal employees have expanded wildly, bringing demands for greater social interference and centralization. (For example, the population in 1900 was about 75,000,000, and there were about 200,000 federal employees; by 1960 the population was about 200,000,000 with about

2,500,000 federal employees.) Increasingly, major areas of concern, such as civil rights, crime, business, labor, and agriculture, transcend local and state boundaries, and the public looks to the only national figure to deal with them. This has been reinforced by the generally dismal performance of state and local governments. They have been particularly reluctant to allow adequate representation to urban interests, which form a major Presidential focus. As the majority of the population shifted in this century to urban areas, the lack of redistricting meant that the President was more representative of the nation's urban majority than were either the state or national legislatures. Moreover, Congressional organization reinforced its parochialism by stressing seniority. The century has watched the continued decline of state and local party organizations, which were the means through which the Presidential nomination could be controlled. Furthermore, the technological developments in communication and transportation, especially since the Second World War, enable the President to go over Congress' head to its constituents. Thus, the growth of routinization and institutionalized assistance for the President has been a response to external conditions, a symptom of a more pervasive set of changes. Those who would cut back the Presidency are really anxious to change the basic sociological, demographic, international, and political trends of the twentieth century.

Beside being irrelevant, such proposals can also be dangerous. Needless to say, a Cabinet composed of legislative leaders when the legislature was not of his party would further weaken a minority President. But the more significant danger lies in the proposal's rigidity, which overlooks the realities of Presidential responsibility. It makes it compulsory for a President to seek advice from a statutory group, while limiting his capacity to seek advice elsewhere. For many reasons this ignores the realities of Presidential responsibility.

There are over 2,500,000 employees in the bureaucracy plus over 2,800 employees in the Executive Office of the President. Among all these millions of individuals only *one* is directly responsible to the electorate—the President.[65] He is responsible not merely for his own actions and decisions, but for everything done by *everyone* of those millions. If someone in the executive branch is charged with sexual perversion, if someone is discovered to have been a member of the Communist Party in the 1930's, if a Peace Corps girl drops an ill-advised postcard where it will offend her host country, if any bureau or agency make errors of judgment, he is responsible, and his public prestige suffers. To protect himself he needs, above all, *information*. That information will not necessarily be available to his staff, which is limited in number and may be limited in perception; yet he must seek out all the advance warnings of trouble he can find. No President can afford to ignore Shakespeare's warning to King John:

> But if you be afeared to hear the worst,
> Then let the worst unheard fall on your head.

To spot the smoke before the fire comes to full blaze, he needs information that may not be available to any routine channel. For that reason, Presidents have never felt obliged to restrict their search for information to one institution. They have turned to sources as diverse as "kitchen cabinets," brain trusts, editors, wives, cronies, and brothers.

The value of varied, informal sources of information is threatened by increased institutionalization. Growth of the formal apparatus is paralleled by growth in the amount of time spent in consultation with its members. Formal consultation absorbs valuable Presidential time and energy. This directs the President's attention to areas of strong institutionalization, leaving him little time for consideration of other areas. President Eisenhower's experience indicated that delegation of this responsibility can only free time at the cost of information, which is even more important to him. Institutionalization brings attendant problems of supervision and a general slowdown in execution and development of policy. It also reinforces the isolation of his office. Thus, he may be handicapped by the very process that enables him to fulfill his routine obligations. Furthermore, his staff may be the object of attack by groups who use them to hurt the President, for example, Sherman Adams for Eisenhower, or Walter Jenkins for Johnson. There is also a strong factor of diminishing returns in the use of staff men. To bargain effectively, they must be perceived by the people with whom they bargain as being close enough to him to know his wishes and have his ear. The greater the number of staff men the more remote they will be and therefore the less believable. He can use only a few men. He needs six men to work a forty-eight-hour day. Forty-eight men working a six-hour day are useless to him, and men capable of working only twelve hour days are nearly as bad.

Presidential responsibility has been rigidified. It would be a dangerous handicap to rigidify his sources of information as well. In the end, it is impossible fully to depersonalize the Presidency because what an individual does with the advice he receives will depend on his perception and political skill. Corwin's Cabinet could not protect America against incompetence, though it could restrict the scope of competence by tying the President to a compulsory group of advisers and limiting his capacity to seek advice from outside sources.

The multitude of proposals for further institutionalization of the Presidency by those who wish to help him are equally ill conceived. These proposals include a second Vice-President for administration, a Super-Secretary to coordinate the various departmental secretaries, giving some other person his respon- sibilities as Chief of State or his responsibilities as Chief of Party. There are also groups that would institutionalize their particular interest by giving him a statutory council of advisers similar to the Council of Economic Advisers in their field, such as education, welfare, and internal security.

Such proposals share similar problems. They do not neces- sarily save a great deal of Presidential time, and they increase Presidential isolation. Adding more men for coordination creates the problem exemplified by Sherman Adams' protectiveness. Transferring roles to other men can hurt the President because of the interdependence of his various functions. If someone else were given the responsibilities of Chief of State, the President would be freed from the Easter Egg roll on the White House lawn, throwing out the first baseball of the season, and meeting deputations of Boy Scouts. But he would thereby be weakened in his capacity to obtain bipartisan support for legislation or to deal as the nation's spokesman in foreign affairs, because he would appear as a partisan spokesman instead of the Voice of the People. If his partisan responsibilities as party chief were

given to another, he would lose bargaining advantages that help
him to obtain his legislative program.

The Presidency is one organ interacting with others within the
American governmental system. Its parts themselves form a sub-
system—a complex, interdependent whole. Zealous reform-
ers are too often like novice mechanics who would remove a
little part that does not seem important, only to discover that
it starts the motor. Reform is difficult because the various aspects
of the Presidential office are so delicately related and exist in
such a complex relationship to the other organs that make up
the total system.

Along with information, the President stands in desperate
need of time.[66] This is the Presidential dilemma, because one
comes at the expense of the other. Either is a costly loss. Let
the reformer beware!

Isolation of Office

The difficulties inherent in maximizing the assets of routinization and institutionalization and minimizing their risks are
heightened by the increasing isolation of Presidential office from
the people for whom the President must act. The city of
Washington is a distorting influence for the perspective of both
the President and his advisers. It is a "company town," and just
as surely as the lives and perspectives of the residents of a mill
town revolve around that industry, the lives and perspectives
of Washington revolve around its "company," the federal
government. There is neither manufacturing nor industry and
hardly any source of employment except either the federal
government or groups who make their living from the federal
government by selling goods and services to its employees or
by lobbying. Most other major capitals in the world have diverse
populations in which a member of the government can immerse
himself. They have business, intellectual, and cultural communi-
ties, which can provide a change of focus for the politician.
Washington has none of these in the sense in which they are
available in London, Paris, Rome, Moscow, Peking, or Tokyo.
New York is the heart of the cultural, artistic, and financial
community in America. The business and intellectual communi-
ties are more diversified, but no major segments are located in
Washington. The Federal City has nothing but politics with

which to engage itself. At parties, at restaurants, at theater or shopping, its residents are surrounded with federal employees. The inside story is the inevitable topic of conversation. Civil servants have lifetime jobs there. The increasing pressures on Congress have lengthened sessions to the point that it is difficult for legislators, especially those with the increased responsibilities that seniority brings, to spend much time in their constituencies. The President and his advisers may have come from a different perspective, but they are quickly ensnared in the center of the web. Technology allows the President to reach more people while he experiences less. Each President has felt escape to Warm Springs, Key West, Camp David, Cape Cod, or the L. B. J. Ranch essential, but this is an emotional release, not necessarily a source of new perspectives.

A President's staff and advisers can be a source of further isolation. There are a great number of men whose careers are dependent on his. The remark attributed to Theodore Sorensen after President Kennedy's assassination indicates this relationship: "he had invested over ten years in John Kennedy's career, and now the investment was gone—gone as surely as though he himself had been the victim in Dallas."[67] All of a President's staff have invested years of their lives in his career and their positions are dependent on his. This fact inevitably colors their advice. They may be so devoted to him that they wish to spare him knowledge of criticism or difficulties within his administration, as Eisenhower's staff did, especially after his heart attack.[68] Because of his indispensability to them they may advise him of his indispensability to the nation as Roosevelt's aides did on the question of a fourth term, although there was good reason to doubt that his health would hold out for the full term. They might simply display the normal hypercaution of the backseat driver or, on the other hand, might promote fights and take a more aggressive line than their leader. Whether consciously or unconsciously, these factors may color the advice he receives.

A final aspect of the isolation of Presidential office which is worth noting is the effect of the office in draining Presidential resources. The sheer exhaustion of office is obvious. It is literally a killing job whose pressures continue to mount. Since 1932 only Harry Truman has walked away from the office unscathed.

Roosevelt died in office, Eisenhower had a heart attack and an operation, Kennedy was assassinated, and Johnson had two operations in his first term. The strain of office is clear in a comparison of photographs of Kennedy at the beginning of his campaign for nomination and those taken prior to his assassination. He had aged perceptibly within a few years.

What is often overlooked is the fact that the pressures on the Presidential staff and advisers have also continued to mount. One reason that there is usually a fair degree of turnover within a Cabinet is the fact that after a few years of these pressures men become physically and emotionally tired in their jobs. They have lost enough battles to know the discouraging limits of the possible. Moreover, the people they must control have learned their weaknesses and operating methods and developed counter-strategies. The enthusiastic crusade has settled into a battle of attrition. The toll of high office on human energy is significant for both the President and those who assist him. This is often reinforced by the difficulty of finding replacements.[69] Any administration enters office with the asset of novelty and hope. If the promise is not fulfilled, and disillusionment sets in, it becomes increasingly difficult to attract able men to an administration. As an administration, even a popular one, nears its end, replacement becomes more difficult because men focus on the new leaders. Whether they hope to profit politically from a President's downfall or prefer to be attached to a rising star, whether they simply doubt his capacity to make the changes they desire or prefer not to be implicated in his disaster, the result is the same—further isolation.

If a President is sensitive to this problem he can compensate in a number of ways. Extensive reading of a variety of newspapers can keep him abreast of many problems. Flexible sources of information, a widespread informal network for gathering information can help, especially if his sources are outside the official governmental hierarchy. Men with the capacity to use information well can minimize the impact of isolation of office, but all will be subject to this draining of resources and isolation as time passes. This combination of public exposure with increasing isolation forms yet another part of the paradox of the contemporary Presidency.

III. Prometheus Bound?

IN SOME DESCRIPTIONS, the President seems almost a Promethian figure whose attempts to aid and comfort mankind have caused him to be chained to the pinnacle of public responsibility while governmental substitutes for the legendary vulture daily tear at his liver. If one chooses to focus exclusively on domestic policies and on the relationship between the President and Congress or the bureaucracy, "Prometheus" indeed appears sorely tried. However, balm may be found for his wounds in a number of factors, including his capacity to dominate the mass media and thus influence public opinion more effectively than any other political actor, his centralizing position in the party system, his legislative leadership, the Supreme Court's practice of legitimizing most innovations in the exercise of Presidential power, and his unique position in the federal system. Chapter IV will analyze the President's role in foreign affairs and defense, to indicate how much further from the tortured Promethian image the President is, outside the area of domestic affairs. This chapter attempts to evaluate the degree to which the President is limited by the other institutions with which he must interact on domestic policies.

CONGRESS

Much discussion of the relationship between Congress and the President presents a distorted picture because it defines power in a highly simplistic manner. One writer claims that the President is too "strong," another that he is not "strong enough," a third that he is "usurping" power, or a fourth that Congress is an archaic roadblock threatening the Republic. At least yearly an article will appear ranking the Presidents by someone arguing that poor Millard Fillmore's "strength" has been overlooked and that he should actually be raised at least to number thirty, whereas Chester Arthur (who has been seriously overrated by the last compiler of such lists) should be demoted to around number thirty-three.

What is often lost in such discussion of Presidential "strength" is a perception that there are two types of governmental power: active power, which comes from being the source of policy initiation and goal setting, and negative power, which stems from exercising a decisive veto on the initiative of another individual or group. Most discussion focuses on the development of Presidential "strength" because he has become the primary initiator in the American political system. It overlooks the manner in which Congress has developed the negative aspects of power. A further distortion occurs because analysis of the relationship between the two branches tends to focus on the decisions that were made. It does not consider those decisions that could *not* have been made. Yet there are many issues that the President does not raise because he knows that they will be totally unacceptable to Congress. In this way Congress often exercises a decisive control over Presidential alternatives—surely a significant aspect of power.

While a detailed analysis of the Presidential-Congressional relationship exceeds the scope of this book, there are several aspects of that relationship which deserve to be highlighted. One is the fact that conflict between the two branches is *inevitable* in the American political system. Beside the constitutional setting of such conflict, both the President and Congress have developed new and imaginative means of exercising influence over the decisions of their rival. Nevertheless, despite these factors, the two branches are functionally interdependent. Each needs the other to fulfill its own role.

Inevitable Conflict

The Constitution assured that the executive and legislative branches would conflict, as a means to avoid governmental tyranny. The philosophy underlying this arrangement was well expressed in *Federalist* 51:

> . . . the great security against a gradual concentration of the several powers in the same department, consists in giving to those who admin-

ister each department, the necessary constitutional means, and personal motives, to resist encroachment of the others. . . . Ambition must be made to counteract ambition. The interest of the man must be connected with the constitutional rights of the place.

In order to assure this conflict, the legislature was separated from the executive, divided into two houses, and each of these three institutions was given a different constituency and term in office, as well as a different purpose for which a different form of organization was most suitable. It is these differences which are mirrored in the decentralization of American political parties.

As has been previously suggested, the Electoral College system forces the President to be particularly attentive to urban, industrial, labor, and minority groups, whereas the Senator's constituency is his state and a Representative's is a far smaller district. Because his constituency is such an important source of rewards and deprivations, each elected official must be attentive to it. Due to differences in scope and diffusion of interests in these constituencies, the demands made by Presidential, Senatorial, and Congressional constituencies differ. Therefore, members of Congress and the President are bound to come into conflict.

The difference in term of office affects the relations between the branches by reinforcing the legislator's dependence on his constituency. Presidential coattails cannot help Representatives during the Congressional elections that fall between Presidential campaigns. Nor are his coattails sufficient to assist a majority of Senators into office because only one-third of the Senate is elected at any two-year period.

This difference in terms has been given added significance by the Twenty-Second Amendment, which limits the President to two terms in office. There is no limitation on the number of terms which a Senator or Representative may serve. Thus, a relative newcomer in the Presidency may be thrown against well-established centers of power. The resulting sense of superiority on the part of the Senate was well expressed by William S. White.

[T]he Presidency has generally sought the expansion of quantitative democracy. . . . [T]he Senate has nearly always sought the preservation

of a qualified and qualitative democracy. To it the movement of time
is of time upon a belt; . . . This is a body that never wholly changes
and never quite dies. This is a "continuing body," where it is actually
harder to change a rule than to vote to take a country to war. To such
a body, where the national past and the national future meet and
soundlessly merge . . . who and what, after all, is a mere transient
President of the U.S.?[1]

Perhaps the greatest source of conflict is the fact that the
two branches perform fundamentally different functions within
the political system. The Presidency must be forward-looking,
geared to innovation. In comparison with Congress, it has
greater assets of unity, speed, secrecy, and information which
make it the inevitable center for military and diplomatic considerations. Congress' function is negative, or restraining. It must
question, debate, and establish a consensus among the various
interests within the society.[2] Standing committees, seniority, and
floor leaders combine with a series of rules affecting every aspect
of procedure and debate to diffuse leadership and underscore
Congress' more negative role.

These differences of constituency, term, and purpose lead to
a willingness to use the checks and balances provided in the
Constitution. They were the "auxiliary precautions," which the
Federalists included to enable ambition to counter ambition.
They entailed an involvement of the President in the legislative
process through his capacity to propose, veto, and administer
Congressional enactments and to appoint Justices and administrators who would be responsible for enforcing them. They also
included Congress' involvement in the executive process through
its powers of the purse and impeachment, its right to declare
war, its capacity to override an executive veto by a two-thirds
vote, and Senatorial advice and consent to all executive appointments and treaties. They have proved an ample arsenal
for Presidential-Congressional warfare whenever provocation
might occur.

Congress vs. the President
In its continuing rivalry with the President Congress has developed a pattern of organization which diffuses power in a deliberate attempt to curtail Presidential interference. It has also

developed means to enhance its position in the formulation of public policy such as the "legislative veto" and legislative oversight of administration.

Congressional organization based on standing committees, floor and seniority leaders, and a complicated system of rules has been a means of self-protection against the President. Nowhere has this been more evident than in the development of the standing committee system. Originally, from 1789 to 1795 there had been a type of ministerial government with each house meeting as a Committee of the Whole.[3] There were no standing committees except a Select Committee on Ways and Means, which prepared estimates. Because Congress was responsible for money bills, the Secretary of the Treasury was given a special relation to the legislature. The act establishing the departments had directed all other executive officers to report to the President, but the Secretary of the Treasury reported to Congress. The first Secretary of the Treasury, Alexander Hamilton, used this as a mandate to breach the separation of powers and dominate Congress. In effect, he superseded the Ways and Means Committee until he left office in 1795. During these years a strong reaction to executive domination had been building in Congress.

On Hamilton's departure Congress developed the standing committee system. This was a system operating on the principle of specialization through a division of labor. Bills were no longer considered before an entire house of the legislature. Instead, each house was divided into standing committees with specialized concerns such as Foreign Affairs, Armed Services, Appropriations, and Ways and Means. (There are at present twenty standing committees in the House and sixteen in the Senate.) When a bill was presented to either house it was sent to the appropriate standing committee, which decided whether to consider it at all, held hearings on the bill, prepared its final form, and presented it to the house for approval. While legislative rules made it possible to force committee action on a bill, they were (and continue to be) difficult to enforce and were therefore used infrequently. Consequently, within its area of competence, a standing committee had paramount power. By diffusing power in this manner, the standing committee system permanently ended the possibility of ministerial government. No longer could any President or his representative dominate either house because its major work was done in many sections.

The standing committee system has led to a diffusion of leadership as well as policy consideration. The party leadership in each house (majority and minority Floor Leaders and Whips) continues to be related to the President in a manner that will be considered shortly. But its control is challenged by the power of standing committee chairmen who influence members of the legislature through their specialized knowledge about a particular subject matter and about the progress of a bill, as well as their capacity to do favors for fellow legislators.

A man becomes chairman of a standing committee by being the member of the majority party in the legislature with the longest continuous service on that particular committee. This recruitment process emphasizes party loyalty only to the degree to which it is necessary for a party to gain a majority of seats in the legislature and gain the initial appointment. Beyond that, continuity of service is necessary which depends on the discretion of a legislator's constituents. If they continue to return him to office, he can afford to ignore his party leaders in the legislature from time to time. If his constituents refuse to return him to office, his party's leaders will be of no help to him. Therefore, constituency demands can be more compelling than those of party for standing committee chairmen. This is reinforced by the fact that long continuous service is generally only possible for non-competitive districts, which tend to be politically stagnant, and therefore unrepresentative of the population as a whole.[4] Consequently, many significant leadership points in the legislature are controlled by men who have only a limited incentive to follow Presidential leadership. He must therefore attempt to bargain and persuade, as he cannot command.

The rules governing legislative procedures may also provide means to thwart Presidential initiative. In the House of Representatives all bills go from the standing committees to the Rules Committee, which is responsible for determining the rules under which bills will be presented to the House. Rules that limit debate and amendment on a bill will be seen by its sponsors as favorable, but bills of which the committee does not approve may be sent to the floor under rules that enable opponents to alter them drastically. The Rules Committee's power also includes determination of which bills will be considered at all, as more bills are reported out of committees than the House has time to consider. This enabled its chairman, Howard "Judge" Smith of Virginia, to fight a very effective delaying action from 1955 to 1966 against civil rights legislation.[5] Although the Senate has no Rules Committee, it has the filibuster, by which opponents of a President's program may seek to delay or terminate consideration of a bill. This has also been used by Southerners to prevent consideration of civil rights legislation. While numerous other rules exist, these are representative of the means available to legislators who wish to thwart Presidential initiatives.

The term "legislative veto" includes various formal and informal committee checks, the use of concurrent resolutions and annual authorizations. Ever since the Marshall Plan, foreign aid has been authorized on an annual basis, and numerous other programs are placed on an annual or bi-annual status. This enables the legislature to check frequently on Presidential performance and cut authorizations where it is dissatisfied. The concurrent resolution is a special resolution passed by both houses to express Congressional sentiment on an issue or event. It has been used to indicate disapproval of Presidential action or to warn him of Congressional sentiment prior to action. Congress may also delay action on Presidential programs, fail to pass them, or pass them in greatly altered versions.

Legislative oversight of administration has grown in importance with the development of the "service state."[6] This function is primarily performed by the standing committees, although there is wide variance in their aggressiveness as overseers. For example, the Joint Atomic Energy Committee has been extremely active and powerful, whereas the Senate Banking and Currency Committee has been more passive.[7] Congressional power to control administrative acts stems from its powers to legislate, finance, and investigate and is reinforced by custom.

Under Congress' legislative powers it establishes and organizes the agencies, bureaus, and departments that comprise the bureaucracy. It is therefore able to abolish agencies of which it disapproves or establish agencies independent of Presidential supervision, such as the Federal Communications Commission and the Federal Trade Commission. It can specify an agency's function in great detail, require the agency to submit frequent reports of its progress to Congress, and limit the sources and qualifications that the President must consider in appointing agency personnel. Congress can also limit his power of removal by the terms under which it established an agency or position. It can specify that the individual may be removed only for cause, and narrowly specify the cause. It can give him a fixed term in office longer than the President's. Consequently, a President's appointment and removal powers have limited significance. This is reinforced by the fact that his powers of appointment do not reach much below the top echelon of the bureaucracy. The vast majority of people in the bureaucracy are civil servants over whose appointment and tenure he has no control. For the leadership positions where his control is greater, his appointment power is checked by the constitutional requirement that the Senate advise and consent to his appointments. The custom of Senatorial courtesy is a further limitation. This custom requires a President to confer with the Senator or Senators of his party from a state before making a nomination to fill a federal office in that state. Customarily he will observe a similar custom of courtesy to a Congressman of his party when appointing a Postmaster for that man's district.

It might also be noted that even in those areas where Congress has left the President a fairly free hand to exercise the removal power, he is limited by his desire not to admit deficiencies in his own administration. Thus, it is more common to work around an ineffective appointee, as President Kennedy did with Secretary of State Dean Rusk, than to remove him.[8]

Congress' power of the purse is another means of administrative oversight. Its appropriation powers permit Congress a means for detailed, continuous supervision of the executive branch. The President's control of agencies through the budget process is weakened by the fact that an agency with support on Capitol Hill can convince the right Congressmen to add money for programs the President does not want and change the Executive Budget to suit the agency's desires.

Its power of investigation is one of Congress' more potent weapons. Ever since the first Congress, legislative investigations have been conducted into the administration of its laws. The need for this oversight was formally recognized in the Legislative Reorganization Act of 1946, which directed that each standing committee exercise "continuous watchfulness" over the agencies under its jurisdiction. In order to accomplish this purpose, the Act provided further staff for both houses, Congressional committees, and a large number of permanent subcommittees. This substantially increased the number of men engaged in review of the executive branch. Since then staff investigation and staff study have greatly developed. The tool of investigation has a great deal of value to Congress, not only in fact, but in prospect. Even when not used, it is a potent threat that brings the bureaucracy into line and keeps it responsive to Congress. Congressional exposés can go beyond questions of corruption or incompetence to more sensitive questions of the policy implications of government action and the misuse of power. All agencies must be wary of this type of challenge.

A number of informal methods of communication between Congressional and agency personnel have also developed, which provide informal methods of influencing administration. One recent study of Congress has suggested that the effect of all these developments in legislative oversight of administration has been to force administrators

> ... to develop a sensitivity to congressional thinking and to try to make their decisions as palatable as possible to those members of Congress interested in agency programs. Congress has become a "court of appeals" in which persons and interests adversely affected by administrative decisions seek redress for their grievances with the bureaucracy.[9]

The significance of all of these developments (Congressional organization, legislative veto, and legislative oversight of the administration) for the President has been their tendency toward insulating Congress from his influence and the capacity they give Congress effectively to exercise the power of policy initiation in its own right. There have been a number of developments in the Presidency, however, to counter these trends.

The President vs. Congress

There are many weapons in the President's arsenal against Congress which have developed or been given new significance within the last few decades. These include his standing with the public, reinforced by his unique opportunities for mass media coverage, party leadership, legislative initiation, and use of the executive veto. He is also aided by some aspects of Congress' rules and organization.

Perhaps the President's greatest asset is his standing with the public. Recent research on political socialization has indicated that children begin to have opinions on the political process at a relatively early age and focus heavily on executives, especially the President.[10] The legislature is normally understood much later than the executive and is generally viewed in an inferior, subordinate role, as a "helper" to him.

The ambiguity of Congress' image has been found to continue into adult life. The complex nature of legislative structure and organization is harder to understand, and it is harder to identify personally with Congress than with the President.[11]

> Of particular significance is the finding that a large portion of the general public evaluate Congress by first assessing the President. Surprisingly enough, this identification is so encompassing that members of the President's party judge Congress more favorably even when it is controlled by the opposition.[12]

The clearest public expectation of Congress' role is that it will cooperate with the President and expedite major aspects of his legislative program.

When this advantage is combined with the President's greater capacity to receive coverage by the mass media and his greater capacity to capture public attention, the tortured Promethian image begins to crumble. Due to the fact that Americans are neither ideological nor politically attentive, the President cannot directly manipulate the electorate through a few fireside chats or television appearances. However, he can highlight a particular issue, communicate his concern about it, arouse some interest group activity on his behalf, and generally set the terms in which the issue will be debated.[13] This is a distinct advantage and one which recent Presidents have actively used.

The President's centralizing position in the American party system has previously been discussed. The broader coalition that he must build to attain office provides advantages over other political actors. The office provides an incentive for party unity and the reconciliation of factions. Equally important is the degree to which the fortunes of a candidate and his Congressional running mates are bound together in an individual district. The separation of terms forces Congressmen and Senators to run for office on occasions when the President does not, but there are an equal number of occasions in which the Presidential candidate will head his party's ticket. In one-party districts where a Congressman has a "safe" seat, that may have limited significance for him, but analysis of the relationship between Presidential votes in individual Congressional districts and the results of House elections has shown that Congressmen whose prospects of reelection are uncertain are heavily dependent on Presidential coattails. The higher the vote for a winning Presidential candidate in a particular district, the greater the likelihood that the district will also elect a Congressman of his party.[14] The consequence of this shared risk in the party label is underscored by research finding that legislators from marginal districts are relatively high in Presidential support scores.[15] This relationship is likely to grow in importance in the future as the number of "safe" districts crumbles under the impact of demographic change and legislative redistricting.[16]

The significance of Presidential leadership for his party's Congressional coherence and unity underscores the problems that the minority party in Congress must face unless the President happens to be of that party. Due to the fact that the actions of a party in power are better known by the public than the words of one out of power, the minority party suffers from a "visibility gap." It can, however, effect public policy if it can form a link with dissident sectors of the majority party, e.g., conservative Midwest Republicans with Southern Democrats.

In 1946 a pioneer study on the source of initiative for major legislation found that the President's role was overrated due to the greater degree of publicity he received.[17] Rather, it was found that most legislation underwent a long maturation process during which individual congressmen had provided the initial proposals and substance. The President played a crucial role in the sense that inclusion of a proposal in his legislative program might be essential for its passage, but it was found that legislative initiative actually came from many sources including sources in the executive and legislative branches, and outside the government.

Within a decade this interpretation was generally passed over as representing the relationship of an earlier era. Instead, political scientists widely accepted the theory that a reversal of traditional roles had occurred during the twentieth century, involving Congress heavily in administration and the President in legislation.[18] It was believed that the President had come to set the legislative agenda, selecting issues for Congressional consideration in his annual Budget and State of the Union messages, and frequent special messages to the legislature, and following Presidential proposals by draft bills formulated in detail within the executive branch. Thus, it appeared that since the Truman Administration, the executive has been the source of both ideas and specific drafts for legislation, and that Congress has come increasingly to play the role of critic, lobbyist for specific programs, or ratifier of Presidential initiative.

Recent research tends to support the earlier description of the relationship between the branches.[19] It would appear that the President is credited with legislative leadership because of the nature of reporting. Inclusion of an idea in his program facilitates public focus on it and may be crucial to its passage. There are, of course, a few areas where Presidential initiative is striking from the earliest stages, rather than just at the stage at which an issue reaches public notice. For example, analysis of the development of the major legislative proposal in the Johnson Administration's war on poverty, the Economic Opportunity Act of 1964, has found that

> The process of shaping the poverty package was legislative in character though executive in locus. Thus, Congress was asked not to draft the war on poverty, but rather, to ratify a fully prepared Administration program, and invited, though hardly encouraged, to propose marginal changes.[20]

Those changes which Congress made in the Economic Oppor- tunity Act were, indeed, marginal. However, a case such as this is relatively rare. Detailed investigation of the antecedents of most major pieces of legislation indicates that Congress con- tinues to play a significant role in the initial stages of formulating policy, despite the annual legislative program, and that this program is frequently a means to highlight ideas that originated with legislators.

Even when the President initiates legislation, it is still Con- gress which must enact it, and Congress is capable of destroying his programs by inaction or damaging them through amend- ment. Thus, Presidential leadership has hardly turned Congress into a simple rubber stamp. It would be a gross distortion to consider the President to be "strong" if there is an implication that his strength must leave Congress "weak." It has greatly developed its negative power and shows signs of continuing in this practice. The frustrations possible for the President can clearly be seen in Kennedy's inability to achieve most of his major legislative goals. In 1963 Congress took no action on three-fourths of his proposals, including his key items: civil rights, tax cut, Medicare, and aid to education.[21] The fact that President Eisenhower had rather limited legislative goals had obscured Congress' growing strength, as did the first few remark- able months of Johnson's Presidency. Johnson's success demon- strated that Presidential power is a possibility, just as is Con- gressional negativism. Yet a fair degree of his success could be attributed to a posthumous tribute to his predecessor, and to his remarkable skill in capitalizing on the temper of the times. The death-wish of the Republican Party gave him such an unprecedented landslide in 1964 that he was able to continue the impression of Congressional weakness for a while, but signs of returning "normalcy" appeared before the mid-term elections of 1966 and were pronounced thereafter. In many major areas of domestic policy he began to face the frustrations his prede- cessor knew. Defense policy is somewhat different and will be discussed more fully in the following chapter. Where domestic policy is concerned, the outlook for the contemporary President is one in which he proposes and Congress often negates or modifies.

However, the annual legislative program has tended significantly to limit the major areas and terms of Congressional debate. This has added importance when considered in conjunction with the President's power to veto enactments of which he disapproves, his party leadership, and popular support. The President's program is also significant for Congress because it gives coherence to the leadership structure and meaning to the role of Congressional leaders, especially in the principal "elective" positions.[22] The Floor Leaders in each house have a mutually dependent set of relationships with the President. They stand at a strategic communication point, serving as an important source of intelligence for the President, but their function within the legislature depends on their ability to communicate his priorities to their legislative associates. The significance of the President's program for Congressional organization can best be seen when the President and Congress are of opposite parties. The "truncated" majority displays much the same unprogrammed, fluid appearance of a normal minority party, whereas the minority party whose member is President generally responds like a majority party within the legislature in terms of coherence and unity.

Further assistance for the President can be found in the very Congressional organization and rules that are capable of limiting him. For example, the diffusion of power in Congress is significant for the President in two ways. As has been noted, it limits his potential for controlling Congress, as was intended. But it also assures that there will be some means of access, even when he is leader of the minority party. There are so many power points that it would be rare for a President to be unable to gain support somewhere in the system. His influence as party leader can be of assistance here. Favorable Senators or Representatives may be persuaded to use the rules on his behalf. For example, liberal Senators can mount a filibuster to prevent passage of a damaging amendment to his legislative request, or favorable chairmen can use all the tools at their command to rush a bill through committee before opposition forces can organize. This was done for the Economic Opportunity Act by Representative Adam Clayton Powell, chairman of the House Committee on Education and Labor.[23] Furthermore, diffusion prevents rival centers of initiative—only the President can coordinate Congress.

Despite their inherent rivalry, cooperation is possible between Congress and the President because they are mutually dependent on each other to fulfill their functions. Because each branch has the means to interfere with its rival through the check and balance system, each must work out accords and build bridges.

THE BUREAUCRACY

Although the President is constitutionally responsible for everything that occurs within his executive branch, Congress has great resources to influence it. Consequently, it is often the battle ground for their rivalry. However, neither branch is invariably able to control the bureaucracy. As a result of twentieth-century developments it has become an independent power in its own right. Two developments have contributed to the bureaucracy's insulation from both Presidential and Congressional control— civil service protections and an explosive growth in the number of individuals involved.

Civil service reform began in 1883 with the Pendleton Act creating a civil service that attained its jobs through competitive examination and could not be dismissed during good behavior. This was a response to the effects on honesty and competence of the "spoils" system which had been the accepted means of choosing public servants from the days of Andrew Jackson.

A civil service independent of external pressure can be an asset for the President in that it is more able to conduct the business of the executive branch honestly and efficiently. Yet it also has drawbacks from the President's viewpoint. At the same time that civil service regulations withdrew the bureaucracy from direct pressure by party organizations, business interests, and some types of Congressional interference, it also withdrew them from the President's direct pressure. He can no longer appoint his partisans to office, nor can he dismiss men at will. Previously, one of his great bargaining advantages with Congressmen had been the patronage at his disposal. As civil service coverage grew, this patronage declined so that currently he has almost no patronage left except some postmasterships and prestige appointments that can be given to representatives of ethnic, racial, or religious groups, or sections of his party, *e.g.*, Cabinet posts, undersecretaryships, and posts in the federal judiciary. Civil service employees have become a separate group organized to bargain effectively with all other elements in the political system.

During the first two decades of the twentieth century the federal government was more active than it had previously been, because defense, foreign relations, and internal improvements were becoming more significant. Yet bureaucratic growth was relatively slow. This changed drastically under Franklin Roosevelt, who initiated the modern "service state" in America. Social welfare and various forms of internal improvements were an essential part of New Deal legislation.[24] Departments grew at a staggering rate as all the new "alphabet" agencies emerged, such as the Works Projects Administration, National Recovery Administration, Tennessee Valley Authority, and Civilian Conservation Corps. Established agencies took a new lease on life, expanding by what seemed almost geometrical proportions. The Second World War and all the centralization entailed in rationing, mobilization, and military necessities added many more individuals to the executive branch. Continued growth in social welfare functions after the War, plus the greater significance of foreign relations and defense contributed to a steady level of growth. Moreover, agencies and departments tended to grow for reasons totally unconnected with governmental needs. Agency personnel, especially at the supervisory level, became committed to the significance of the task they were doing and wished to protect the project. Interpersonal and interagency rivalries played a part in promoting the desire for empire building. There was no need to fear that additional personnel would not be used—Parkinson's Law reminds us that "work expands to fill the time allowed for it."[25] The result could be as ludicrous as the development of the Department of Agriculture, which has continued to grow during a period of rapid decline in the farming population. If present trends continue it is possible that by the 1980's there might be more members of the Department of Agriculture than farmers in America!

In 1900 there were approximately 200,000 members of the federal bureaucracy. In 1960 there were approximately

2,500,000 members. Due to the inherent tenacity of any established administrative system, they are not likely to undergo major reduction or change. Although President Eisenhower was more fully committed to reduction of the bureaucracy than his Democratic peers, his battles were in vain—it continued to grow. Lyndon Johnson's economy move of a bureaucratic "job freeze" on further hiring also made little impact. This condition poses grave difficulties for Presidential *or* Congressional supervision, making the bureaucracy in many respects a headless fourth branch of government.

Struggle for Supervision

To whom are the various administrative agencies which compose each department responsive? From whom do they receive their leadership, supervision, and control—and in what degree? The answer to these questions underlies the struggle for supervision, because the constitutional setting is ambiguous. It provides overlapping spheres of power to the Executive and Congress, which intensifies their rivalry. An observer who was discussing the relationship between Congress and the President with regard to the bureaucracy once noted,

> Whatever else can be said about the Washington scene, it is not neat. The centers of power are many; the patterns of cooperation and conflict are loose and ill defined. They are also tentative.[26]

The existence of this rivalry creates an area of ambiguity into which other elements step, in hopes of exercising at least limited direction and control. These include the career staff, courts, interest groups, communications media, the party organizations and other agencies.

Actors Attempting to Influence Bureaucratic Policy[27]

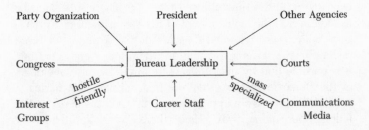

Despite formal administrative theory the career staff (civil servants) exercises an important element of control over bureau leadership, because it has a monopoly on the information with which bureau leaders must work. By its decision on what and how much a bureau leader must know, it limits his decisions. Career staff must try to make rational calculations of what information their leaders should receive, based on aspects of the situation and the leader's personality. With reference to the situation any bureaucracy develops a "don't rock the boat" syndrome. He who "makes waves" is not generally given the department's more interesting work nor recommended for rapid promotion. If a penalty is placed on showing initiative, or transmitting painful information to their superiors, bureaucrats may be concerned for self-protection. Such responses can have serious cumulative impact on governmental policy. With respect to their leader's personality, they must calculate what he will do with the information they send up the line of command. For example, if they know that the bureau leadership is looking for any excuse to end a project about which they are deeply concerned, they will be hesitant to furnish it. These career staff members may have worked for several decades in an area of high leadership turnover and may wish to hide previous mistakes or prevent the new leadership from making what they regard as new ones. Whatever the motivations, and myriad others could be suggested, the career staff has the ability to control bureau policy in many ways by its choices on the type and timing of information it will transmit.

The courts have a far more limited impact on the bureaucracy, but not an insignificant one. Bureaucratic decisions or methods can be taken to court. For that very reason, the "don't rock the boat" syndrome causes bureaucrats to try to stay carefully within the letter of the law. Fear of litigation reinforces already hypercautious tendencies. Even for those bureaus that are not subject to litigation as a rule, great weight is given to advisory opinions by the Department of Justice on the legality of proposed action.

Both friendly and hostile interest groups are likely to try to influence a bureau's policy. They can try to bring pressure to bear directly or indirectly through influence with key Congressmen, the party, the mass media, other agencies, or the President.

Their impact depends on their size, financial backing, and support in other areas of the governmental structure or with the public. For example, the American legion has strong public and Congressional support as well as a large membership and treasury. Its opinions, therefore, carry great weight with the Veterans Administration. Farm laborers' unions are small, poor, and low-status, whereas organized farmers enjoy the reverse situation. For this reason, against their rivals, the laborers enjoy far less access to the Departments of Labor and Agriculture.

The communications media include both mass and specialized media. Each can have significant impact on the bureaucracy. The Federal Bureau of Investigation is an example of an agency for which the mass media are particularly significant. J. Edgar Hoover has developed the FBI into an autonomous branch of government completely independent of Congress, the President, or the Department of Justice of which it is ostensibly a part. The Bureau's prestige is so great that Hoover can damage anyone who tries to tamper with his control. Understandably, for four decades he has always been the first man appointed by any new administration (although most other bureau leaders are changed), and he was given an indefinite extension of his term of service when he reached the age of mandatory retirement. He has created this position by careful cultivation of the mass media. To do this he cultivated a reputation for high effectiveness, which had its costs. To maintain this reputation it was necessary to limit the areas in which the FBI would operate, and as far as possible to avoid cooperating with other law enforcement agencies. Furthermore, it has avoided any role that leads to conflict with local police agents because these are a source of useful information for law enforcement in a locality and of political support. The result of Hoover's success through the mass media is that the Bureau is independent of every form of control except that of the mass media, but it must sustain its reputation for high effectiveness if it is to maintain this independence. Perhaps that was why Hoover felt so threatened by criticism of the Bureau's role in the Kennedy assassination that he responded by publicly and heatedly criticizing the Warren Commission report.

The Bureau of Geodetic Survey in the Interior Department

is an example of an agency for which the specialized media are particularly significant. The national press of America is unlikely to give sustained attention to this Bureau's policy. In fact, the mass media are largely unaware of its existence. Certainly, the general public is unlikely to rush to newsstands to buy magazines or papers for feature articles on the way the coastline is mapped. However, the *Geophysical Journal*, which services the small community of American geologists, is interested. It has an impact on Bureau policy because it helps to form the opinion of the influential men in the field which that Bureau serves.

Other agencies within the bureaucracy may also be involved in the struggle for supervision. Because there are overlapping jurisdictions, more than one federal bureau may be involved in a given question. Because different bureaus have developed different basic constituencies, different operating procedures, and different outlooks, conflict is likely. For example, conflict often occurs between the Army Corps of Engineers and the Bureau of Reclamation over irrigation policy.[28] The Bureau of Reclamation cannot build irrigation projects for farms that exceed 640 acres. If more than half of the project can be labeled as flood control, the Army Corps of Engineers can build irrigation projects for farms of any acreage. Naturally, the Corps is favored by large land owners. There is a jockeying for position between the two federal agencies, with the Corps trying to get the Bureau to admit that a project is primarily flood control, whereas the Bureau tries to avoid having this designation applied.

The last and least potent line of supervision is provided by the party organization, which seeks placement and preference for the faithful. It is limited by civil service requirements to the degree that the faithful must be able to pass the civil service examination. However, in some areas there is room for discretion in placement and therefore more room for party pressure. This is particularly important in the Post Office Department and in the Department of Justice (*e.g.*, district attorneys, federal marshals).

The significance of constitutional ambiguity and the multitude of actors trying to influence bureaucratic policy is that no one in the system has enough power to act alone. The bureaucracy cannot be controlled by the President, Congress, or any of the extra-constitutional actors involved. Therefore, alliances have to be worked out. Alliance building becomes a dominant characteristic of the system.

A paradoxical rule thus governs the struggle for supervision.[29] The President must dissociate himself from the bureaucracy because he cannot involve himself physically in all its activities, and to avoid overidentification in case of failure. Therefore, the agencies are forced to seek protection elsewhere—in alliances with interest groups, Congressional subgroups,[30] or with the public (*e.g.*, FBI and the mass media). The most successful way for a bureau to deal with the struggle for supervision is to form a "cozy little triangle" through established accommodations between the bureau, its organized interest groups, and the chairmen of the relevant subcommittees.[31] If the President tries to bring pressure to bear, the agency can rush for its two supporting partners. If Congress gives it trouble it rushes to the other side of its triangle, the organized interest groups (and may incidentally try to play the President off against Congress as well). Some bureaus are in the ideal position of having a divided interest group support, which enables them to capitalize on the divisions and to rise above the fray independent from *every* means of supervision and control. For example, the Forest Service has two interest groups, which will unite to support it against Congressional or Presidential interference, but which it can play off against each other. (Cattle, lumber, and mining interests want access to national forest land, while conservationists, hunters, and fishermen want to limit access.) Thus, bargaining rather than command characterizes the relationship between the President and "his" bureaucracy.

The only agencies or bureaus that are dependent on the President for support and therefore amenable to his supervision are those which are at a disadvantage in the broader political system. He is always given the uphill fights, such as protection of the Bureau of Reclamation or the United States Information Agency. The Veterans Administration has its cozy little triangle with the American Legion and the standing committees on Armed Services, or the House Committee on Veterans Affairs (which has no Senate counterpart). The various bureaus in the Agricultural Department have their triangles with organized farm groups and the standing committees on Agriculture. Organized labor groups and the standing committees on education and labor form support for the various bureaus of the Labor Department. A bureau has to be politically "orphaned" to be totally dependent on the man whom Americans hold responsible for the entire bureaucratic structure. An example of such a situation is the Children's Bureau in the Department of Health, Education, and Welfare. It has no political friends, nor any particular organized group support, and has traditionally experienced the anomaly of being headed by a spinster. The dependence of such a bureau on the President is hardly likely to be viewed by him as a political asset.

In order to assert his personal control the President obviously has to try to split up the cozy little triangles while keeping at least one step ahead of his bureaucratic opposition. Yet the triangles can only be split if the President can build his own alliances and make his own bargains with one or more of their elements. Such support comes at a price that he may be unable or unwilling to pay.

To keep ahead of his bureaucratic opposition the President must keep informed of the disputes, controversies, and problems arising within his executive branch and must convince his subordinates that both their action and their failure to act will be known to him. This requires great administrative skill. Obviously, the most disastrous way to deal with the question is to delegate responsibility to a Chief of Staff. That results in profound ignorance of the bureaucratic situation on the President's part, enabling bureaucrats to disregard Presidential wishes.

The most successful modern President in asserting personal control over the bureaucratic structure was Franklin Delano Roosevelt in his first term. He used a number of techniques to stimulate conflict within the executive branch, and out of these clashes (*e.g.,* Ickes *vs.* Hopkins) he gained valuable insights into bureaucratic trouble spots and alternative policies. However, the contemporary President is more limited in the techniques which he can use.

While President Roosevelt was able to engage in selective immersion in a particular set of administrative operations or policy decisions, contemporary Presidents must work on deadlines and are less free to set other things aside for a while. President Roosevelt was more free than contemporary Presidents to seek alternative sources of information to supplement those in the formal, official structure. The contemporary President has been forced by the developments of institutionalization and routinization to be more of a reactor to deadlines set by others than an actor, and to be tied more closely to official sources.

Another technique that President Roosevelt employed was that of appointing competitive personalities in overlapping jurisdictions. This is still an important technique, but it is less useful for the contemporary President because the personalities at the top of the federal agencies have less impact than was the case when government was smaller. Also, the development of formal consultation between bureaucratic groups can steal a march on the President by coming to accords through which they can present a united front on policy or organizational matters. Thereby he loses the learning advantage of public conflict.

Fundamentally, it is impossible for the President to exercise complete control over his bureaucracy. Other pressures are stronger, and the techniques of the past have less relevance. Although it is a weak reed to support his hopes, one major asset is his capacity to develop personal loyalty among the bureaucracy. This is only possible if he can communicate his desire to hear the tough problems and uncomfortable information. If he can transmit a desire to support those men who exert initiative and imagination, he may develop loyalty among them. Obviously, if all he learns about their actions comes in a daily blurb from a Chief of Staff, the normal conservatism of a bureaucratic structure will prevent men from rocking the boat. Nevertheless, although bureaucratic loyalty may help a President over some rough spots, it cannot fundamentally change the fact that in the struggle for supervision he is at a disadvantage.

The Cabinet

It would be comforting to the President if, in the midst of his uneven struggle, he could look to his Cabinet as a nucleus of allies, but it lacks power as an institution, and the individuals in it can offer only limited aid.[32] The ambiguity of their position prevents them from playing the supportive role that is theirs in theory. They must be his advisers, yet at the same time each heads an executive department. This subjects them to pressures different from those on the President. They can be useful to the President because they represent other interests, but for that very reason they cannot be depended upon as a source of bureaucratic control. Their loyalty must be divided. Anyone who heads a department must accord respectful attention to rival voices, even if he personally desires nothing more than serving the President.

Unfortunately for the President, such desire is rare. He must appoint men to his Cabinet for reasons quite different from their personal loyalty to him. He must consider factors of "balance" in terms of geography, religion, and ethnic background (race may soon be added). He must consider "appropriateness" for the job in broad terms, for example, New Yorkers are unlikely to be selected Secretary of Agriculture, whereas Kansans have little hope of being Secretary of Labor. He may have to use the job as a reward for the nomination or election support of a key party leader. Several factors may cause the President to select someone who is not his first choice for the position. The drawbacks of public office keep many men from accepting appointment, as do factors of age, health, and family responsibilities. An appointment must receive confirmation by the Senate, whose antagonism to an individual must be considered and may prevent the President from proposing some names. There is, after all, a limit to the crusades a President can hope to handle successfully, and he may prefer to place his emphasis on substantive programs rather than individuals.

A final factor assures that he will not receive complete aid and comfort from his Cabinet members—their personal political ambitions. If a Secretary hopes for a further political career, especially if he hopes to attain the Presidency itself (e.g., James Farley, Henry Wallace) he will have to differentiate himself from his Chief. It is understandable that Presidents would turn to advisers outside the formal, institutional structure such as kitchen cabinets, brain trusts, old cronies, or relatives.

THE SUPREME COURT

The Supreme Court has always been aware of its institutional vulnerability and its lack of coercive power. Therefore, it has acted with particular circumspection toward the President. After an extensive analysis of the relationship between the two branches, Glendon Schubert wrote, "It should be perfectly obvious by now that the most significant aspect of judicial review of presidential orders is its ineffectiveness."[33] The Court has made enough decisions on the margins of Presidential power to indicate that it has not completely abdicated, but its general approach has been quite permissive. On the other hand, the President has had a significant impact upon the Supreme Court and the entire federal court system through his power as chief law enforcement officer. It can be argued that his influence on the Court is more significant than its influence on him.

Definitions of Presidential Power

The Supreme Court's major relation to the President has been that of *legitimator* of his power, especially in foreign affairs and defense. It has allowed the President what is tantamount to absolute power in his roles as Chief of State and Commander-in-Chief, which includes his capacity to proclaim the existence of a national emergency as well as engaging in acts of war. In foreign affairs he alone has the power to speak or listen as a representative of the nation.[34]

Only in the domestic sphere have his powers been limited, and there only if the action is not keynoted to his emergency powers. For example, President Truman's action in seizing the steel mills to prevent a strike that would have hurt the economy and endangered the Korean War effort in 1952 was held unconstitutional because Congress had prescribed remedies through the Taft-Hartley Act for such a situation.[35] Had his emergency power not been so defined in this situation, his interpretation of the extent of his powers might well have been accepted. The only point on which the Court has been consistently anxious to limit Presidential action has been seizure of property. Individual liberties and freedom can be dealt with summarily under a claim of emergency power. As Glendon Schubert has suggested, the Court's impact on the President's domestic action is not likely to grow, because the number of Presidential actions of domestic impact which are not keynoted to emergency powers is disappearing. The very limited effect of judicial review on Presidential action can be judged from the fact that in the nation's history only fourteen decisions have held Presidential orders unconstitutional, and a third of these decisions came before Grant's Presidency.

One area in which Court decisions have had most impact on the President is in his role as Chief Administrator, because the Court has restricted his removal power. Departing from a precedent established by Chief Justice William Howard Taft (a former President) which had given the President complete power of removal,[36] the Court declared that his removal power was not "illimitable." It held that during their prescribed term he could not remove officers of a body that exercised quasi-legislative and quasi-judicial functions, such as the Federal Trade Commission, except for one or more of the causes named in the statute that established those offices.[37] Later, his power of removal was confined strictly to officials who were part of the executive establishment, but not members of a body that was created to exercise its judgment without hindrance, unless Congress had explicitly conferred this power upon him.[38] At present, then, he may only exercise his removal power over those officers whom he has appointed within the executive branch such as Secretaries, Undersecretaries, and bureau heads. Therefore, the Court has upheld Congress' power to limit the President's removal power.

The President as Chief Law Enforcement Officer

The Constitution asserts Presidential responsibility that the laws be "faithfully executed." This requirement underscores the Supreme Court's weak position, because the Court has no means to execute its own orders but must rely upon other political actors. Andrew Jackson's apocryphal announcement that "John Marshall has made his decision, now let him enforce it!" suggests how a President can sabotage a Court order by inaction. But the context also demonstrates the limitations upon flouting Court decisions. Jackson's remark followed a case involving interpretations of a treaty with the Creek Indians in the Southeast. State land laws had violated the treaty, and Marshall held state laws void, on the grounds that the treaty was meant to protect the Indians. An old Indian fighter, Jackson sympathized with the states and refused to enforce the Court order. He could do this because there was no real pressure on him to enforce the law in any meaningful political terms. Indians could not vote, and white men were not about to protect them against the greed of white land speculators. The President would, in fact, have had an extremely difficult time enforcing Marshall's decision, if he had wanted to.

Generally, however, the President is under pressure to enforce Court orders. During the intervening 140 years the Court has established itself firmly as an important part of the system of checks and balances. While Americans may grumble about individual decisions, they usually respect the Court as an institution and therefore prefer to prevent it from being interfered with. President Roosevelt learned this to his sorrow in 1937 when he proposed the Court-packing plan. It is therefore unwise for a President openly to defy the Court. Moreover, Court orders usually involve groups that have far more political power than the Creek Indians. The President's freedom in this area depends, essentially, on the expectations that are focused on him. If his constituency and other political actors expect him to comply with Court orders, his options are limited. Even though he might prefer to avoid encounters such as those with Governor Faubus at Little Rock in 1957, Governor Barnett at the University of Mississippi in 1962, or Governor Wallace at the University of Alabama in 1963, he could not, because there was a general expectation that he would enforce the Supreme Court's desegregation decision. This often has serious political consequences for the President because it removes his flexibility and forces him to be a key figure in a script written by his enemies. Faubus, Barnett, and Wallace increased their political standing by seeming to protect their states from external foes. The better the President fought, the more political mileage they got, whereas each confrontation provided a political risk for the President in that it had the potential for loss of face in his national constituency.

Although it is rare for a President to be able openly to flout Court orders, differences in willingness to act have a great effect on Court rulings. A President may slowly comply with the bare letter of the law or may go far beyond it in his zeal. For example, there was a significant difference in enforcement of the Supreme Court's desegregation decision under Presidents Eisenhower and Kennedy. Eisenhower never explicitly stated support for the holding in *Brown v. Board of Education* and did nothing actively to encourage compliance with it.[39] His stand at Little Rock was a necessary response to protect the Presidential power that had been tied to the Court order. During his administration there was little deliberation and less speed concerning integration. President Kennedy entered office with enforcement of this decision as an explicitly high priority. His brother was given responsibility in this area, and the Department of Justice was given a newly organized and expanded civil rights section. The Department actively sought examples of failure to comply with Court orders and brought cases under them. Although the promised land was not at hand for race relations, integration speeded up appreciably.

Like all grants of authority, the President's responsibility to enforce Court orders may be either a risk or an asset, depending on the degree of routinization involved. It can be an asset because it legitimates his intervention in a wide variety of situations, but it will be more of an asset if he has really flexible choices. If strong expectations exist he must take action, and under those circumstances it may prove to be a risk. The "take care" clause does not mean anything precise because there is a range of discretion and choice in any administrative system as to the way a law will be administered.

There is another way in which the President exercises great influence on the federal court system—his appointment power. He is responsible for appointing all federal judges at each of the three levels: Federal District Courts, the Courts of Appeals, and the United States Supreme Court. By the kind of men he appoints he affects the character of the system. Judicial appointments have a lasting impact because men are appointed for life during good behavior and may serve for a quarter of a century or more. Their longevity may be gathered from the fact that over the same period of time there have been ninety Congresses, thirty-six Presidents, but only fourteen Chief Justices. Presidential appointments affect the judicial system in three ways. If the President selects men who are in agreement with his philosophy their interpretation of the law may reflect this. Federalists packed the judiciary in their final hours before extinction as a political party, leaving constitutional interpretation in the hands of men like John Marshall. For thirty years Marshall protected the Constitution from the philosophy of Jeffersonian and Jacksonian Presidents. When Franklin Roosevelt was finally able to appoint men to the Supreme Court, he quickly secured a majority favorable to New Deal measures.

A second, more subtle way appointment influences the court system is in the intellectual capacity of the men who are appointed. If the President merely considers the judiciary as a form of patronage to reward an old family retainer, as the Kennedy family intended before Francis X. Morrisey's appointment to a Federal District Court in Massachusetts became too controversial, the whole federal legal structure will suffer. If a man's capacity for judicial office is less important than factors of balance or patronage or friendship, court decisions are likely to be incompetent and lead to a chaotic legal system.

A final way in which Presidential appointments may influence the entire question of taking care "that the laws be faithfully executed" is through the personal willingness or refusal to act on the part of the federal district judges. For example, *Brown v. Board of Education* left enforcement of the desegregation decision to the local federal district judge. President Kennedy's concern for civil rights was belied by his appointment of several conspicuously ardent segregationists as federal district judges in the South. The most prominent of these was Harold Cox of Mississippi, who long after the President's death continued to make mockery of enforcing the desegregation decision or any other in that area.

CONSEQUENCES OF FEDERALISM

The federal context within which the President must operate proves both a strategic weakness and a tactical advantage for him. It limits his strategies in that the decentralization of the political system must always be an important element in the construction of his legislative program and his relations with his party's leaders. It provides guidelines on the areas where he will have to make concessions and forces upon him a diplomatic role in his relations with fifty semi-sovereignties. Nevertheless, the states are not his direct concern. His subordinates have to face the operating problems of federalism more than he.

The tactical advantage the President receives from federalism is the singularity of his position within the American political system. Because power is diffused among fifty states and the national legislature is composed of men who are not nationally elected but represent those states and the localities of which they are composed, he and his Vice-President are the sole nationally elected figures. This not only gives him special stature with his own party and in his relationship with Congress, it increases his stature at the expense of the opposition party. Federalism ensures that there cannot be a national opposition leader with any equivalent political base. All political opposition to the President must come from men whose base is at the state level, primarily Governors or Senators. Consequently, opposition leaders are less visible to the national public than the President, and less able to gain a public hearing. As one scholar noted: "The blurred public image of Congress is . . . further blurred, and the already monumental disadvantage of the out party made worse, in the television age."[40] President Johnson even attempted to co-opt the governors by bringing them in for periodic policy briefings and pep talks in a manner reminiscent of the uses Presidents have made of bipartisan consultation on defense or foreign policy. Those who were implicated in policy formulation were at a disadvantage for later criticism. This was a fact painfully learned in 1967 by Governor George Romney of Michigan, whose prestige was severely damaged when he tried to reverse his earlier support of administration policies in Vietnam on the grounds that he had been "brainwashed."

The primary effect of federalism is to force the President into a dissembling role, because the American people are only "instrumentally" in favor of federalism. The very groups and individuals who speak of "states rights," and the need for "limited" government are the first to retaliate if the federal government tries to restrict its programs or limit its spending in areas of which they approve. For example, farmers' associations speak glowingly of the independence of the sturdy yeoman farmer but demand the extension of parity payments and various federal agricultural programs. The American Legion staunchly joins the American Medical Association against Medicare while enjoying one of the world's most complete systems of socialized medicine in the Veterans Administration hospitals, which provide all services from induction to the grave. Southern governors curse Washington while at the same time demanding federal funds for road, school, and hospital construction. Even a candidate as stoutly devoted to the concept that "the government is best which governs least" as Ronald Reagan had to undergo a rapid education into the realities of Californian desires for governmental services. When Barry Goldwater offered the alternative of returning to dependence on the states and cutting federal services, the shockwave reverberated through every voting booth in the land.

Fundamentally, the majority of the American people are no more willing to live by their theories on the value of limited government than on their theories that all men are created equal, or that liberty and justice should be provided for all. Therefore, once aroused, the President must defer to their prejudices against strong government but find ways to circumvent those prejudices when they want action. Above all, he must keep their eyes off the pea he is shuffling under the walnuts because they demand to be fooled. They want incompatible things, and they do not want to be told this. All peoples live by myths—this is an American version.

Conclusion

The constitutional resources of Congress to check and balance Presidential power in domestic affairs have been supplemented by developments in Congressional organization, veto power, and oversight of administration, thereby creating an impression that "Prometheus" is heavily bound. While these restrictions should not be minimized, the President gains significant leeway and bargaining advantages from his standing with the public, his centralizing position in the American party system, legislative leadership, legitimization of his powers by the Supreme Court, and his unique position within the federal system.

Strong bonds exist, however, which are unknown to the Constitution. They result from the capacity of his bureaucracy to absorb and deflect Presidential initiatives. While no President will be able to overcome this handicap entirely, one with sensitivity to the uses of Presidential power, administrative skill, and the sense of direction that is more fully discussed in Chapter V will at least be able to limit its impact.

IV. Prometheus Unbound?

PPROMETHEUS was finally freed of his torture through Hercules' intercession with Zeus. To some observers the President's shackles would seem to have been removed through the demands of defense and foreign policy. For example, fear of the consequences of such apparent freedom was vividly expressed in a report of the Senate Foreign Relations Committee investigating America's involvement in Vietnam.

> Already possessing vast powers over our country's foreign relations, the executive by acquiring the authority to commit the country to war, now exercises something approaching absolute power over the life or death of every living American—to say nothing of millions of other people all over the world. There is no human being or group of human beings alive wise and competent enough to be entrusted with such vast power. Plenary powers in the hands of any man or group threaten all other men with tyranny or disaster. . . . The concentration in the hands of the President of virtually unlimited authority over matters of war and peace has all but removed the limits to executive power in the most important single area of our national life.[1]

Certainly, foreign relations and defense are the areas in which Presidential influence is agreed to be predominant. While the public also views others (such as legislators, Governors, or spokesmen for interest groups) as legitimate to formulate domestic policy, the President is accorded primacy in matters of defense and foreign affairs. Congress has become more a lobbyist for particular programs than the active check envisioned in the Constitution. The Supreme Court has legitimized the President's definition of his own power in these areas. Yet preeminence does not equal freedom. The President does not initiate personally but chooses among the alternatives presented to him. Successful initiation in defense or foreign policy must include him, which is the measure of his power. He is *the* necessary member of any innovating group in defense or foreign policy, yet he is heavily dependent on the information and alternatives presented to him by his advisers. The more power the President attains, the more influential the bureaucracy becomes.

Since World War II both foreign and defense policy have undergone bewildering shifts and realignments that have changed the context within which the President must function. The Second World War permanently ended America's century and a half of isolation, inaugurated the Atomic Age, and set the stage for an East-West confrontation. In doing this, it completely changed the context within which American foreign and defense policy were made, with significant implications for the nature of the Presidency.

FOREIGN POLICY

Any separation of foreign and defense policy must be somewhat arbitrary because of the growing interrelationship of the two. Nevertheless, there remain sufficient differences in objectives and personnel to warrant separate consideration.

The President's primary asset in influencing American foreign policy is his standing with the public, which puts any opponent at a severe disadvantage. Other assets stem from his constitutional powers, customary developments, and informal means of influence. While Congress has some means of resistance, the primary limitation upon the President is the nature of the State Department and the degree to which he can exercise control over its personnel and that of the Central Intelligence Agency.

Public Opinion and Foreign Policy
Public opinion is related to the President's role in foreign policy with regard both to the nature of public opinion concerning foreign policy issues and to the nature of public opinion concerning the President's foreign policy role. All analysis has shown that American public opinion concerning foreign policy issues lacks intellectual structure and factual content. In the leading study on American voting behavior it has been suggested that

> In general, people pay much less attention to political events and issues
> than is commonly realized. . . .Many people fail to appreciate that an
> issue exists, others are insufficiently involved to pay attention to recog-
> nized issues, and still others fail to make connections between issue
> positions and party policy.[2]

While this statement has general application to all public policy
issues, the authors found it particularly true with regard to
questions of foreign policy. There it was possible to find some
recognition of partisan differences when questions were presented at "the simple global level of getting into war or staying
out of it," but these quickly "faded out when the issue grounds
were shifted to the more specific *means* of attaining the goal."[3]
In studying the variations in levels of intensity of involvement
with regard to foreign policy questions, V. O. Key found a
mixture of realism with a romantic longing for withdrawal from
foreign affairs. This carried over into a "puzzling mixture of
bellicosity and friendliness in our responses to the alien world."[4]
Opinions favoring a "tough line" toward the Soviet Union or
Communist China were fairly intense, but the intensity of
opinion supporting foreign aid was particularly low. The lack
of intellectual structure implied by these findings has produced
a reaction to foreign policy questions which is one of mood,
unstable and subject to manipulation. This has been reinforced
by the lack of factual content in American public opinion
concerning foreign policy. Studies have consistently found that
most Americans have a generally low level of information about
international affairs. This has often been attributed to a lack
of available information, or a lack of education, but neither
explanation is entirely persuasive. In large urban areas where
there is a great deal of information available on international
affairs, a majority of individuals still show no knowledge of it.
A recent study of the differences between the college educated
and the general public found that there were far greater simi-
larities than advocates of education would appreciate. While
the college educated had more opinions than the general public,
"their opinions were based on incomplete information and
possessed the . . . emotional quality" of opinions by the general
public.[5]

The more persuasive explanation for the general lack of

intellectual structure and factual content on foreign policy may be found in the remoteness of these questions from the experience and knowledge of the majority of individuals. Questions of domestic policy are obviously more directly relevant to individual experience, which leads to greater knowledge about their probable effects and consequences. Moreover, American foreign policy has become so intimately connected with defense policy that there has of necessity been a cloak of secrecy over large areas of information critical to the formulation of foreign policy. This has denied the public information on which to base intelligent decisions and has emphasized the remoteness of international affairs from everyday interests and activities. In analyzing public opinion polls, Gabriel Almond found two facts of particular importance:

(1) the extreme dependence of public interest in foreign affairs on dramatic and overtly threatening events; (2) the extraordinary pull of domestic and private affairs even in periods of international crisis.[6]

Nevertheless, all is not flux where public opinion on foreign policy is concerned. There are certain basic opinions that fix the limits within which foreign policy must be formulated, and which have a relatively high stability.[7] Obviously, the primary attitude is loyalty to the United States and hostility to any nation that threatens it. Since World War II a broad consensus has also developed supporting American participation in world affairs (as opposed to the isolationist consensus that dominated American thought until the Second World War). Finally, there are relatively stable gradations in public attitudes toward other nations. For example, Canada, Ireland, or Norway are always viewed in a highly favorable light as compared with Russia or China. Within this framework, there is a wide leeway for choice on foreign policy alternatives.

However, it would not be correct to conclude that because public concern about foreign policy is superficial and unstable, those who have responsibility for its formulation experience few limitations. Government officials are affected by what Carl Friedrich called the rule of anticipated reactions. They are constantly concerned about the potential reaction of the American people, the press, and especially what Gabriel Almond termed the "attentive public," which is not hesitant to voice disagreement with government policy and to work through the mass media to create widespread dissatisfaction among the less attentive. The President and his advisers are continually wary of potential response to their actions. Nevertheless, the public tends to provide a President with substantial leeway in this area.

A consideration of the nature of public opinion concerning the President's foreign policy role demonstrates how much he is favored over other elements in the political system which are engaged in foreign policy formulation. A recent study has found that a representative sample of Americans desire "a man who is strong, who has ideas of his own on how to solve problems, and who will make his ideas prevail even if Congress or the public should oppose him."[8] Because the public also fears abuse of power, it wants the President to be restricted to eight years in office, but for the duration of office, it was found that the public preferred to abdicate any responsibility for foreign policy decisions to him. This support is heightened by crisis situations (presumably even when the President is to blame for them). Respondents explained their reaction on the basis of a lack of knowledge and information on their part, as opposed to the President's superior ability and knowledge and their trust that Presidents would not abuse this power.[9] However, when questions concerned Presidential power on domestic issues, this support was sharply reduced.

Presidential Tools

Presidential strength in foreign affairs rests initially on powers the President has always had. As Chief of State he controls all official contacts and procedures in foreign relations. This means that he has sole responsibility for negotiation and maintenance of lines of communication with foreign powers. Among all the actors in foreign affairs he has the greatest legitimacy and greatest presumed expertise, or command of expertise. Besides his institutional sources of information (e.g., the State Department, Central Intelligence Agency, Department of Defense), the President can get a great deal of information from the press if he chooses to. He can use other individuals or groups as fact finders or spokesmen, such as the Vice-President, Senators or Representatives, friends in communications or business, or members of the White House Staff. With this variety of information and presumed expertise, others who come into conflict with him are at a disadvantage.

Beyond his powers as Chief of State, the President benefits from responsibilities more recently attached to his office. For example, his roles in setting the Congressional agenda and leading his party in Congress can be used to particular advantage by a skillful President. This has resulted in a steady decline over the last two decades of Congress' capacity and opportunity to innovate in the area of foreign policy. Its function has come to be primarily one of modifying, negating, or legitimating proposals that have originated in the executive branch.[10] Because the President sets Congress' agenda through his State of the Union message, Budget message, and special messages throughout the year, and because technical drafts of legislation are now prepared in the executive branch, Congressional innovation in foreign policy has steadily declined in all but marginal areas.[11] The President sets the topic and tone of the foreign policy debate for Congress through these powers. The inadequacy of Congressional organization to the formulation of foreign policy contributes to this decline. Congress is well designed to consider narrow, individual aspects of foreign policy, but poorly organized to set long-range goals and handle broad policy considerations. Congressional organization is more adequate to the formulation of domestic policy. In the area of foreign policy it has been said that

> . . . Inventive problem-solving requires . . . *integrative* solutions. The decentralization of Congress, however, does not lend itself to ready integration of specialized knowledge—indeed, some Congressional subcommittees are so autonomous that their decisions are rarely reviewed, much less reversed, by their parent committees. Moreover, the knowledge of a few individual experts is not a sufficient foundation for public policy decisions. . . . Because it is organized more or less bureaucratically, the executive branch is in a much better position than the legislature not only to absorb and comprehend vast amounts of data, but also to marshal information in the manner required for policy-making by its leadership.[12]

In addition to his advantages in information and setting the Congressional agenda, the President also benefits from his position as party leader. This role creates a further degree of Congressional dependence on his initiative. Thus, when the majority party in Congress has a President of its own party, it tends to shift to an internationalist position.[13] This occurred among Republicans in 1953 and among Democrats in 1961.

There are a number of specific tools that the President can use against Congress to enhance his advantageous position on foreign policy formulation. Among these are bipartisan foreign policy, Congressional joint resolutions, draft treaties, executive agreements, tacit understandings with foreign powers, foreign aid, and movement of men and materiel through his power as Commander-in-Chief. Ostensibly, bipartisan foreign policy is a means to consult leaders of the opposition party. Actually, if he is skillful and ruthless enough, a President can use it as a means to reduce Congress' capacity to act meaningfully on foreign policy issues. Congressional leaders are usually consulted too late to look fully into the alternatives. An extreme example of this occurred during the Cuban missile crisis when President Kennedy consulted Congressional leaders at five in the evening and made his speech to the public at seven. While more time is usually available, the consultation is frequently only a briefing, hastily arranged to tell Congressional leaders what the Executive intends to do or to try to obtain acquiescence on something that has already been done. Because opposition leaders are thereby implicated in the policy, they are limited in later debate. The stake that the President's own party has in supporting him means that the only consistent source of opposition or criticism to his policy could come from the leaders of the opposition. Thus, bipartisan foreign policy can be a means to silence some of the President's most responsible critics.

Another Presidential tool for control of foreign policy is the Congressional joint resolution giving advance approval to actions the President may deem necessary. This was first used by John Foster Dulles in January, 1955, in the "Formosa Resolution," which gave the President the right to defend the off-shore islands of Quemoy and Matsu near the Chinese mainland. Such joint resolutions have been used by Presidents as blank checks to justify a wide area of action. The most obvious example of this was the use President Johnson made of the Tonkin Gulf Resolution of August, 1964, which he requested after American ships in the Gulf of Tonkin reported having been fired upon by North Vietnamese patrol boats. The Resolution gave the President approval for taking "all necessary measures" to repel armed attack on American forces, and to "prevent further aggression," and "all necessary steps, including the use of armed force" to assist any SEATO nation asking help.[14] It was used by the President as an authorization to send a half-million men to Vietnam and to bomb near China's border. Due to the sweeping manner in which President Johnson used that resolution, Congress has been wary of giving him another such tool. In April, 1967, he wanted to go to the conference of American leaders at Punta del Este, Uruguay, with a Congressional promise of "significant" financial support for the creation of a Latin-American common market. While the House passed such a resolution, the Senate, under the leadership of J. William Fulbright, balked at providing a blank check to circumvent appropriation procedures and therefore passed a watered-down version. Significantly, many Senators offered to ram the resolution through the Senate again if the President so desired, and if he had wished to fight, there is good reason to believe that he could have obtained acquiescence.

Draft treaties provide a further means through which the President can create commitments which are particularly difficult for Congress not to honor. While the Senate is responsible for advising and consenting to all treaties drafted by the President, his drafts are well publicized before reaching the Senate. Therefore, in the eyes of other nations the United States is committed to the policy when its Chief of State has made such a commitment. It is rare for the Senate to subject the nation to the international "loss of face" that failure to confirm such a treaty would cause. Such an action would hinder any President in further international transactions by undercutting international confidence in his capacity to speak for his nation. It would therefore have far-reaching and serious implications for the conduct of America's entire foreign policy.

Rather than treaties, the President can write executive agreements, or enter into tacit agreements with foreign powers instead of written ones. *He* creates commitments or involvements, then asks Congress whether it will back the commitments of *the United States of America*—there is a formidable slide from "I" to "we."

After the First World War general public sentiment favored isolation and conceived of the Senate leadership as at least as legitimate a spokesman in foreign affairs as the President. That is no longer the case. The President can now subject a recalcitrant Congress to intense public pressure by going over their heads to the country. The political difficulties in rejection of draft treaties or Presidential commitments are therefore severe. Moreover, any responsible Senator must consider the consequences to America's international position if Presidential initiative is not supported. In case Senators should show any tendency to forget this, it can be brought to their attention in various ways by Presidential assistants, as occurred with the Test-Ban Treaty. Once negotiated, it is very difficult for a Senator to cast the deciding vote to kill a treaty.

A President can also commit the United States to a particular foreign policy through his power as Commander-in-Chief. His capacity to move men and materiel is significant here, as is his greater power of leverage against Congress where defense appropriations are concerned. For example, Congressional sentiment in 1940 was adamantly isolationist, and unwilling to take any stand but one of neutrality toward Great Britain and the Second World War. As Commander-in-Chief, President Roosevelt was able to negotiate the exchange of fifty overage destroyers for bases in the Caribbean which assisted Britain and helped to prepare America for what he knew to be an inevitable involvement in the War.

Perhaps Congress' most consistent means to oppose Presidential initiation in foreign policy occurs through its power of the purse. It has been particularly insistent on cutting foreign aid appropriations through the years because public commitment to foreign aid is slight. This is indicated by a table showing the differences between amounts of foreign aid requested by the President and actual Congressional appropriations for foreign aid over a ten-year period:

Foreign Aid Cuts (in Billions of Dollars)[15]

Year	Requested	Appropriated
1958	3.86	2.77
1959	3.94	3.45
1960	3.93	3.23
1961	4.87	4.43
1962	4.77	3.91
1963	4.78	3.90
1964	4.53	3.00
1965	3.52	3.25
1966	3.46	3.22
1967	3.35	2.94

Although Congress' capacity to cut foreign aid requests is admittedly a significant limitation on the President, it is not as great as would appear from the figures. Obviously, in formulating budget requests it is possible to take into account the likelihood of Congressional reductions and request more funds than necessary, in order to provide some bargaining leeway. Furthermore, Congress has limited impact on the way in which these funds are administered. Through the Bureau of the Budget, the President can direct uneven distribution or impounding, as has been previously discussed. Moreover, cuts in foreign aid appropriations have less impact than is generally realized because frequently they are at least partially restored in later, less publicized supplemental appropriation bills. In fact, the President's power in foreign relations is emphasized by the whole question of foreign aid—despite its lack of popularity in Congress and with the public at large, several billion dollars a year are regularly appropriated for it at his insistence.

This discussion of Congress' relation to the President on foreign policy formulation would seem to support Roger Hilsman's analysis of the decision-making process.[16] He suggests that there are concentric rings of decision-making in foreign policy. The innermost one is composed of the President and the men in departments and agencies who must carry out the decision. The middle ring is composed of other departments in the executive branch, and other layers within the agencies and departments already involved. The outer ring is composed of the "public arena," *i.e.*, Congress, the press, interest groups, and the "attentive publics." Most major decisions in foreign policy are made within the innermost ring, and there Presidential initiative can be the determining factor. This is not to imply that he is the sole policy maker, but his is the controlling voice in foreign policy. For others who wish to have their ideas accepted, it becomes necessary to obtain at least his acquiescence, preferably his active support.

Presidential Liabilities

On individual foreign policy issues Congress can exercise a decisive veto. For example, Presidential initiatives have been rebuffed on questions of Russian consulates in the United States, East-West bridge building, or Roger Hilsman's China policy. However, they are not the major limitation envisioned by the check and balance system. The greatest limitations for the President in formulating foreign policy come from his own executive branch, particularly in the structure and personnel of the Department of State and the Central Intelligence Agency, and from any personal inadequacies in attracting able advisers and making intelligent use of their advice, which he may have. To an able, sensitive President, the institutional problems can be most frustrating.

Four characteristics limit the State Department's usefulness for him: the complexity of its organization, its cautious habits of thought and practice, its lack of institutionalized support, and the types of contacts it makes.[17] The extreme complexity of its organization leads to general passivity. Because it spreads across the world with overlapping lines of authority, it is difficult to coordinate policy at all. It is nearly impossible to coordinate innovation. This complexity reinforces its extremely cautious habits of thought and practice, which have been further reinforced by various traumas suffered during the Joseph McCarthy era. Identification with foreign policies that turned out to be wrong or unsuccessful was considered not merely an error but grounds for suspecting one's loyalty. A considerable number of career foreign service officers were driven out at this period. As a result, State Department officials learned that policy identification could be dangerous in some later post mortem. If, for example, one wrote the wrong memo on Cuba in 1961, his career would be in trouble. This encouraged writing opaque communiques and very guarded assessments of the situation in any given country. It reinforced the typical bureaucratic habit of telling a superior what he wants to hear, or confirming policies already decided on. The instinct for playing it safe is far greater in the State Department than in any other area of the bureaucracy because a mistake may be considered not just a matter of bad judgment, but of disloyalty. If a person in the State Department is going to have any policy identification, only one is safe—hard line anti-Communism. Being first to scent danger puts one among the angels. In any post mortem one is safe, because if wrong, his error is ascribed to patriotism. This reduces the meaningfulness of field reports from State Department officials, because there is only one safe side on which to err. The degree to which the State Department gives in to these pressures is created by the third factor, its lack of institutionalized support.

Among the American public there is a general lack of sympathy for the State Department, its personnel, attitudes, and functions which strikingly contrasts with the position of every other major element of the bureaucracy. As has been suggested, most parts of the bureaucracy have the support of an array of powerful interest groups, and there are predictable broad coalitions they can form (their "cozy little triangles"). The Defense Department can mobilize support from veterans or defense-related business organizations; Treasury has the financial and business community; Commerce has the National Association of Manufacturers and the Chamber of Commerce; Labor has organized labor; and the Department of Agriculture has organized agricultural interests. This type of widespread institutionalized support does not exist in foreign affairs. The State Department has some interest group support such as the Council on Foreign Relations, but these groups lack the widespread base and public appeal of the interest groups related to other major departments.

The public is generally distrustful of a department part of whose function must be to represent the attitudes of others to the United States. This antagonism is intensified in many parts of the country by a class envy based on an inaccurate public image of all State Department personnel as being sophisticated, Eastern, upper class, and ivy league. This feeling was capitalized on by Senator Joseph McCarthy who coined the epithet "cookie pushers from Harvard." He was able to make such successful inroads on the State Department precisely because it lacked broad public support. His tactical error came in shifting focus to the Department of Defense.

This lack of public support for the State Department leads to a concern for pacifying its enemies. It is an appeaser—not of the foreign enemy, but of its domestic critics. For example, John Foster Dulles put Senator McCarthy's prime ally, Scott McLeod, in State Department personnel and security control and let him dismiss widely as a means of appeasement.[18]

The State Department's usefulness is further limited by the fact that its contacts are almost entirely with existing governmental leaders and social and economic elites. It is therefore frequently unaware of or insensitive to antagonistic leadership. This means that in nations where the existing regime does not receive popular support (as in many countries of Latin America) United States' contacts are with the more reactionary elements and are perceived as such by forces in the country striving for social change. Consequently, the information upon which the State Department formulates policies may be inadequate, and the contacts it has had with a previous regime may inhibit the establishment of useful relations with a revolutionary successor.

All four of these factors limit the State Department's usefulness for the President. It has thousands of individuals engaged in operations and procedures but not in developing policy initiatives. As President Kennedy discovered to his sorrow, it is not a piece of effective governmental machinery, but a "bowl of jelly," which absorbs attacks by yielding. He is reported to have wanted to keep it as a facade but actually to have thirty well-trained men to do the work.[19]

Another Presidential tool that is hardly an unmitigated blessing is the Central Intelligence Agency. Although this group is not supposed to have a foreign policy, it creates foreign policy problems. It is concerned with both information gathering and policy formation, and there is little coordination of the two.[20] While cloak and dagger routines comprise only a small part of its function, they are disproportionately likely to cause foreign policy repercussions. Its liabilities to the President stem primarily from its built-in tendency to see conspiracy and to assume that the appropriate way to deal with the threat is counter-subversion. It is not likely to see other alternatives. There may also be bias in the manner in which it collects its estimates, as was shown by the Bay of Pigs fiasco. The CIA did not gather intelligence from all groups of Cuban exiles, but only from those with whose political ambitions for the island they were in sympathy. Unfortunately, the "leftists," who were thereby excluded, had better contact with the underground in Cuba and were better informed on actual conditions. A further problem with CIA operating procedures is its emphasis on the personalities of individual leaders. Allen Dulles was quoted as saying: "Oh, he would never do that. I know him." The fallacy of this approach lies in the fact that individual leaders are not free to function entirely according to their preferences. They must work within the framework of their institutional setting and the goals, personalities, and power of their competitors for policy making. A Russian leader devoted to detente may be forced to a hard line if his military advisers can gain the support of key party leaders, just as President Roosevelt's personal commitment to internationalism was ineffective in the face of a strongly isolationist sentiment in Congress and the country at large. The President is heavily dependent on the man who is CIA Director, because it must be a secret, tightly organized hierarchy. Therefore, there will not be men who can step outside the chain of command to inform the President of any problems, as is possible in other agencies. Despite all these limitations, the CIA has not been dismantled because its functions are necessary. Above all, it is a source of information and contact with groups in each country which the State Department is institutionally incapable of reaching.

To a large degree a President sensitive to these limitations and the nation's needs in foreign affairs can compensate through developing informal channels of advice, attracting capable advisers, and using their advice intelligently. Consequently, the

greatest limitation on a President in foreign affairs is the limitation of his own perceptions. If he has a sense of direction and
is decisive and politically courageous, he can leave a significant
body of accomplishments in foreign relations. This is shown in
the contrast between the Truman or Kennedy contributions and
those of Roosevelt, Eisenhower, and Johnson.

Until World War II President Roosevelt had lacked any
general principles on which to make foreign policy decisions
and had, therefore, improvised from situation to situation, with
contradictory or nebulous results.[21] President Truman aimed,
instead, at establishing a long-range foreign policy based on
helping Europe to rejuvenate its economy and maintaining
freedom from Communist domination. Because of the priority
he gave these objectives, he submerged personal and partisan
considerations, inaugurating a fruitful period of bipartisanship
in foreign policy formulation. Through the aid of men like
Secretary of State George Marshall, Under-Secretary of State
(later Secretary) Dean Acheson, and Senator Vandenberg, President Truman was able to provide bold, imaginative, durable
countermeasures in the Cold War including the Truman
Doctrine, its logical extension in the Marshall Plan, Point Four,
the European Recovery Program, the North Altantic Treaty
Organization, and the Berlin Airlift. Any one of these might
be considered a departure from previous foreign policy patterns.
Taken together, the impact was most impressive. Each suggested
a willingness on the part of the American people to respond
to the world crisis in an imaginative manner. His role in foreign
affairs was summarized:

> . . . as President he wrought the boldest and most far-reaching changes
> in United States foreign policy of any President in history—changes
> which have markedly affected the destiny of the world ever since.[22]

This high point of creative foreign policy was brought to a
sharp close by American failure to comprehend changes in the
non-Western world, especially the Far East. Failure in America's
Far Eastern policy brought the end of bipartisanship and inaugurated the McCarthy era of intense bitterness and self-
distrust. As Gabriel Almond has suggested, these developments
led to the deterioration of American foreign policy:

. . . The collapse of Nationalist China in 1949 and the outbreak of the Korean War in 1950 broke the back of the bipartisan alliance and created a mood of distrust which deepened as the costs of the Korean War were driven home by the draft, casualty lists, military budgets and taxes. This was the mood that was played upon by the right wing of the Republican Party to create . . . a threatening myth of an international Communist plot which had penetrated all the institutions of American society. . . . Our foreign policy turned into a hard shell of military production and deployments, security diplomacy, and a program of foreign aid that was assimilated into our security diplomacy. The image we turned to the world was contaminated by internal distrust, arrogant self-righteousness, and shaky nerves productive of boasts and threats.[23]

A President with a more flexible, imaginative response to foreign relations might have minimized the impact of this era on foreign relations, but his previous military career had prepared Eisenhower to view foreign relations primarily in terms of defense. More important, he stood in awe of his Secretary of State, John Foster Dulles, and tended to rely so heavily upon his opinion in matters of foreign policy that he seemed often to have abdicated the field.[24] His Secretary was a man of absolute self-confidence and moralistic fervor, who tended to see the world in simple terms of black and white, enemy or ally. The result was a hardening and narrowing of American foreign policy. The only significant new ideas in foreign policy were extensions of the NATO compact principle, i.e., SEATO, ANZUS, CENTO, and OAS. Earlier innovations, like the Marshall Plan and NATO, were continued but brought into line with the new policy.

During this decade of increasing inflexibility in American foreign policy substantial changes were occurring in the international context. The death of Joseph Stalin in 1953 spurred a far reaching series of alterations in the Communist world. Within the Soviet Union there were important shifts in internal structure and policy as well as in foreign policy. Tensions and divisions within the Communist bloc which had been obscured under Stalin's dictatorship began to alter the once monolithic structure of international communism. Outside the Communist bloc as well as the Western bloc a "Third World" of newly emerging nations in Asia, Africa, and Latin America was developing. It had aspirations and needs separate from those of either America or Russia and could not easily be placed in the simple dualism of Dulles' policy. These differences were often expressed by an explicit policy of non-alignment.

There were many important Republican spokesmen for change such as Senators Cooper of Kentucky and Aiken of Vermont, or Governor Nelson Rockefeller of New York, but as long as President Eisenhower left foreign policy formulation almost entirely to his Secretary of State, and that Secretary had a sense of personal infallibility, little change was possible. The result was a "significant gap between challenge and response in our conduct of foreign policy."[25]

President Kennedy was particularly sensitive to this gap. He entered office determined to meet the challenge of the international context by a tough-minded pragmatism that based a flexible foreign policy on a realistic assessment of the world situation. His policy emphasized helping new nations to strength and independence through economic and social progress. This led foreign aid into new directions, away from military and technical assistance toward an organized promotion of national development such as land reform and education. Kennedy made clear his determination to exercise the controlling voice by his appointment of Dean Rusk as Secretary of State. Both Roger Hilsman and Arthur Schlesinger maintained that the President expected leadership qualities from his Secretary, but if so, that is surprising judging from the personal characteristics of Rusk which each author described. Schlesinger reported that:

> He was, more than anything else, a man bred in the large organizations of mid-century America. But unlike McNamara, his organizational instinct was for service, not for mastery. . . . He seemed actually to prefer stale to fresh ways of saying things. . . . He was a superb technician: this was his power and his problem. He had trained himself all his life to be the ideal chief of staff, the perfect number-two man. . . . He had authority but not command.[26]

Hilsman summarized Rusk's impact on foreign policy by quoting a critical newsman:

> There are two facts about Dean Rusk that are revealing. The first is that he was Assistant Secretary of State for Far Eastern Affairs during the Korean War. The second is that no one even remembers it.[27]

Whatever President Kennedy's expectations may have been, during Dean Rusk's entire period of service to Kennedy not a single policy was associated in the public mind with his name. Kennedy was definitely in control.

To America's allies and the Third World, President Kennedy was a hopeful symbol of a new era in American foreign policy. While his record in foreign affairs was not uniformly successful, it would seem to have justified their hope. The complexity of Asian problems did not admit of easy solutions, but he made valuable contributions by neutralizing Laos, considering Vietnam primarily a political and social problem rather than a military one, effecting some improvement in relations with Indonesia (ended when Sukarno turned on the Federation of Malaysia), and developing a more flexible approach to China at the time of his death. His policy of a Multilateral Nuclear Force was more of a gimmick than an effective new policy for Europe, and the Alliance for Progress in Latin America had developed some serious weaknesses before his death, but his tough-minded, pragmatic approach paid handsome dividends in the Cuban missile crisis and in Africa. As Schlesinger wrote; "In no part of the third world did Kennedy pioneer more effectively than in Africa."[28] The aftermath of the missile crisis was a detente in relations with the Soviet Union which led to the Nuclear Test Ban Treaty of 1963 and further easing of international tensions.

President Johnson's contribution to foreign policy produced an uncertain pattern. On the one hand, there was an attempt to continue basic Kennedy policies such as the Alliance for Progress, and the detente with the Soviet Union. His accomplishment of a treaty with Panama in 1967 opened a fresh path in an area marred by long strife between the two nations. Nevertheless, his policy toward Asia and the Dominican Republic suggested less flexibility and a greater concern with satisfying his domestic hard-line critics. Changing the basic conception of the Vietnamese problem from a social and political question to a military one was symptomatic. To some degree this could be attributed to his preference for working through established departmental channels. A State Department headed by Dean Rusk provided a vacuum into which Secretary of Defense

McNamara rushed. Rusk had consistently "failed to stand up and make the case for the political side . . . with the strength, vigor and determination with which Secretary McNamara and the military chiefs made the case for the military side."[29] Kennedy could compensate for this through dependence on other resources and his own experience in foreign affairs, but Johnson lacked these assests. His personal staff did not provide the resources in foreign policy which Kennedy enjoyed, nor had he an adequate personal background. His most serious weakness in foreign policy was even more directly related to the uncertain pattern of his decisions in this field:

> He had no Johnson policy or Johnson philosophy to guide him. . . .
> one close friend . . . described him as a 'nationalist' . . . in the sense
> that his first interest was national, not international, affairs.[30]

Clearly, in his choice of William Rogers as Secretary of State President Nixon indicated his intention of being his own Secretary. Rogers had no particular expertise in this area, whereas many other Republicans had, for example: Senator John Sherman Cooper of Kentucky, Governor Nelson Rockefeller of New York, or former Governor Willian Scranton of Pennsylvania. Nevertheless, from President Nixon's viewpoint William Rogers was preferable because he was a close personal friend whose judgment the President trusted. Lacking an independent political power base, he was entirely dependent on the President. Thus, he provided loyalty and energy while the President intended to keep the reins of State Department policy in his own hands. It is too early to assess the impact of this policy, but it would seem likely to encounter many of the same problems that Kennedy faced following a similar strategy. However, some of Kennedy's difficulties with the "bowl of jelly" may be overcome because William Rogers is a more effective administrator than Dean Rusk.

In summary, the President's greatest need in foreign policy is information and intelligently presented alternatives from which to choose. The institutional characteristics of the Department of State make it difficult for a President to obtain either from it. Much of the daily activity in foreign relations occurs at levels of the bureaucracy below his immediate advisers. The

President's impact must therefore come through his sense of direction and purpose, and his sensitivity to the limitations of his institutional advisers.

MILITARY POLICY

Just as in foreign policy, the President dominates military policy making because it is he who defines an issue and sets forth the choices. Although he, personally, may not be the source of military policies, his acquiescence, at least, is necessary for any policy to be accepted. As in foreign policy, successful initiation must include him. He dominates the choice of strategic programs and, growing out of that, decisions on the size of the defense budget, the organization of the military and defense establishment, and the development of weapons systems. Public opinion is even more highly supportive of his commanding role here than in foreign affairs, and Congress poses even less of a limitation upon him. As Professor Huntington has demonstrated, the whole process of policy formation on strategic programs tends to occur within the executive branch, which then implements its own decisions.[31] Thus, the primary limitations on Presidential initiative in military policy are similar to those in foreign policy: the perceptions of his advisers and his own perceptions. Two further limitations affect military policy, connecting it to the domestic sphere—the politics of fiscal policy and the difficulty of terminating military involvements.

Public Opinion and Military Policy

Since the Second World War, general public opinion in America has consistently supported large military forces. As V. O. Key wrote, "The scarcity of genuine pacifists means that the defense establishment does not have to fight for its existence."[32] The preference of the general public for a large military force is supported by the "attentive public" in military affairs: veterans' groups, Army and Air Force Associations, Navy League, defense-related industries, and every community that may be threatened by the shutdown of a defense installation.

Since 1950, public opinion has never favored reduction in the country's military strength.[33] In fact, it has been found that whenever governmental policy and mass opinion differed, the general public favored more military effort than the administration. Even when the sensitive issues of increased taxes or unbalanced budgets were posed as the likely results of military spending, the public supported a high level of military spending—even *in peacetime*.

More important for the President than the general public attitude toward military policy is the public attitude toward his role in its formulation. Here there is widespread acquiescence in his decisions. One example of many polls on the subject found that seventy-five per cent of those interviewed believed that if he felt it necessary, the President should send troops abroad even if *"most* Americans are opposed to sending troops there."[34] Although mass opinion prefers a large military force, it acquiesces so completely in the decisions of the administration that the public will support a reduction of military force after the administration has carried it out. The President is therefore able to project his own goals and values onto the public, as he determined what they want. For example, the economy drives that reduced military spending in 1948–1949, 1953–1954, and 1957 were justified by Presidents Truman and Eisenhower on the ground that "the public would not support" a large military establishment. Actually, there was no indication prior to these announcements that the public would not support it. However, the President's announcement functioned as a self-confirming hypothesis: "The public and the communications elites look to the Administration for leadership of defense matters; they interpret such a statement to mean that the public should not or need not support a large defense effort."[35] Public opinion, therefore, supported reductions in military spending. As Samuel Huntington has demonstrated, this presents critics of reduction in military strength with an insoluble dilemma: before they attack the administration the majority of the public would favor their viewpoint, but once they have brought the problem to the public's attention the administration will reassure the public, and it will be converted. "By initiating a debate over defense the critics insure that they will lose the debate."[36] Whatever democratic theory might prefer, acceptance of the President's controlling position in the formulation of military policy is widespread, cutting across sectional and socio-economic lines, and fairly constant. Any limitations upon him must come from other sources.

Presidential Tools

Despite constitutional delegation to Congress of the power to declare war, to raise armies, and to finance military policies, the President has come to exercise decisive power in these matters, as well as matters of military structure and strategy. A summary of just a few executive decisions since the Second World War indicates the breadth of Presidential influence:

> . . . The executive decided whether the Air Force should have 95 or 137 wings, the Army 14 or 24 divisions, the Navy 200 or 400 warships. The fundamental decisions to maintain a massive nuclear retaliatory force, to construct a continental defense system, and to develop or not to develop forces for conventional limited wars were all made in the executive branch. The decisions on whether to build hydrogen bombs, "supercarriers," long-range jet bombers, intermediate-range and inter-continental ballistic missiles, nuclear-powered submarines and planes were also executive decisions. This is not to say that congressional groups played no role in these decisions. In a variety of ways they could influence them, and in some cases compel the Administration to pay a high price to get what it wanted. But they could not make the decisions. The effective, final "yes" or "no" rested with the executive branch.[37]

The President's decisive role in determining matters of military structure and strategy may be seen from a brief review of major developments after the Second World War. President Truman was solely responsible for the decision to drop atomic bombs on Japan, which ended the War. In the ensuing surge of euphoria the huge military machine with which the War had been waged was dismantled with reckless abandon. At the end of the War American uniformed personnel numbered 13,000,000. By February of 1948 it numbered 1,009,000, including 631,000 ground troops, of which 253,000 were on occupation duty. The remaining 378,000 men were all that were available to cover the hot spots of the globe.[38] The decision for such rapid and total demobilization had been taken by President Truman on the strength of military estimates that it would be a decade before any world power would be capable of warlike action and the the American monopoly of atomic power gave the nation an unassailable position. However, disagreements with the Soviet Union in 1945 and 1946 made the government fully aware that Stalin was no "noble ally" and that it would have to oppose further Communist expansion. Therefore, the policy of "containment" was first publicly stated in the Truman Doctrine, and in George Kennan's "The Sources of Soviet Conduct" in 1947. But containment required a strength that America lacked, due to demobilization. Furthermore, the American nuclear monopoly ended in September, 1949, with the first Russian atomic explosion.

Changes were clearly required in all aspects of military policy. Structural problems had to be dealt with, relating to the intense interservice rivalries. Here President Truman had mixed success, but later Presidents were able to further his intentions. The Second World War had been waged with frequently disturbing conflicts between the Navy and War Departments and the Army Air Corps, which had its own interests. In 1947, with Presidential initiative, the military system was reorganized to provide three separate services, ostensibly coordinated within a Department of Defense. However, the first Secretary of Defense, James Forrestal, had little success in his initial attempts to unify the services. In that same period the National Security Council and Central Intelligence Agency were established, and the groundwork was laid for a more meaningful unification, although that did not occur for some time. The well-developed bureaucratic structures of the military services resisted change diligently.

Far more important than the debate on structural changes was that on change in military strategy. What were the appropriate force levels, weapons, and alliances? Should the United States rely on a capacity for massive retaliation, or must it also develop capacities for more limited war? Above all, how could the conflicts between domestic goals and military spending best be resolved?

In 1950, on Presidential direction, the National Security Council thoroughly reviewed American military strategy and determined that the most appropriate goal was the development of free world capabilities and cohesion on the basis of the

Council's findings.[39] President Truman instituted a crash program for rearmament, based on an assumed date of maximum
danger in ten years. However, Korea proved many American
strategic theories to be unrealistic. Americans had been oversold
on air power, and it soon became apparent that this was at most
a secondary factor, while ground action was still primary.
Chinese Communists demonstrated that they could match
American technical capacity by superior tactical flexibility.[40]
Nuclear weapons did not bring the military invincibility that
many Americans had expected, because they were weapons of
mass destruction, ill-suited to field tactics. Moreover, the possibility of nuclear war made the concept of "victory" meaningless,
since in a fundamental sense all sides would be losers. As one
general remarked, after a nuclear war the survivors would envy
the dead. Therefore, it became necessary to return an element
of rationality to warfare. This was only possible if its objectives
and means were strictly limited. The price of limiting warfare
was limited victory.

To a nation accustomed to the concepts of "total victory"
and "unconditional surrender" this was a frustrating, bewildering novelty. Nevertheless, President Truman decided not to risk
escalation of the Korean conflict into a Third World War and
therefore commanded American forces to limit their objectives
and weapons. This was not a decision that found general acceptance among the public or in Congressional and military circles.
The Supreme Commander of American forces in the Far East,
General Douglas MacArthur was among those who found it
unacceptable. His insubordination on this point caused the
Commander-in-Chief to dismiss him from his command in one
of the most controversial actions of the Truman Presidency.[41]
Yet, despite public and Congressional uproar, when the dust
settled, one of America's most honored military heroes was on
the sidelines, while the President retained command of armed
forces responding to the directive of limited warfare.

On entering office, President Eisenhower instituted a "New
Look" at military strategy, which essentially accepted the goals
of the Truman Administration but revised the crash program
of rearmament into a permanent program for the "long pull."
The actual effect of this revision was to reduce the pace and

scale of rearmaments in the interests of economy. There was a renewed emphasis on tactical and strategic nuclear weapons on the ground that this would provide a "bigger bang for the buck." However, this heavy reliance on atomic weapons posed one serious problem: they were the only American response available for a range of conflicts from a mob stoning the United States Information Agency to the bombing of New York City. The threat became less persuasive as the scale of the conflict declined relative to the costs to the United States. Clearly, the United States would not use nuclear weapons on the mob, nor on many such relatively small-scale threats.

President Kennedy decided upon a shift in military policy. Under the guidance of Secretary of Defense, Robert S. McNamara, and General Maxwell Taylor, both structure and strategy were fundamentally changed. The Defense Department exercised greater unification and coordination over the rival military units, and cost efficiency was coupled to diversified capabilities. In order to structure a variety of forces to be able to meet a wide range of situations and crises, the conventional service boundary lines became irrelevant. Therefore, mixed forces were developed, organized around various kinds of strike commands and responsibilities. As a consequence, service lines were downgraded. Also under Kennedy the Special Forces were established to fight guerrilla warfare with greater skill and flexibility than conventional forces allowed. These changes provided a more diverse, but also a much more expensive, defense establishment.

All of these decisions on military structure and strategy were formulated and carried out within the executive branch. Many more could be cited to indicate the major point: that Congress can no longer exercise the balancing role that was expected of it by constitutional theory. Specifically, its three great powers to declare war, to raise armies, and to control the purse have an increasingly limited impact on Presidential decision-making.

Congress' power to declare war is obsolete because the President can send troops to battle irrespective of any declaration, as was done in Korea and Vietnam. Because he makes the choices on deployment, he is the one who takes the nation to war or chooses to avoid it. All that Congress' power amounts to is an acknowledgment of an existing situation. For example, after Pearl Harbor, Congress could hardly have avoided a declaration of war on Japan. More important, it has become a facet of diplomacy in an era of limited war *not* to have a declaration of war. In August, 1967, Congress was told by Under-Secretary of State (previously Attorney General) Nicholas Katzenbach that its constitutional power to declare war was "outmoded," because it was inappropriate to a limited war fought for limited objectives and could even risk expansion of the war if resorted to. He pointed out that in Vietnam the Tonkin Resolution and SEATO Treaty gave the President "as broad an authorization for the use of armed forces . . . as any declaration of war . . . could be in terms of our internal constitutional process." Then he rubbed salt into Congressional wounds by announcing that the President had not actually even needed the Tonkin Resolution because "he already had constitutionally that authority."[42] This testimony merely underscored that hard fact that whereas Congress might have *de jure* power, the President has it *de facto*.

This statement angered many members of Congress, particularly Senator J. William Fulbright and a number of members of the Senate Foreign Relations Committee, of which he was chairman. Their growing frustration over the President's conduct of the Vietnamese War led to a marathon television debate in March of 1968 in which Committee members tried to secure an assurance from Secretary of State Dean Rusk that the administration would consult with Congress before sending additional troops to Vietnam. After ten hours of testimony by the Secretary, Senator Fulbright was reported to have said wearily, "He never did answer us on whether there would be consultation before a decision is made."[43] Congress has the capacity to request Presidential consultation, but it lacks the power to command it.

The power of the purse lacks its original significance because the President has the power of deployment and sufficient stockpiles of war materiel to involve the nation in armed conflict before he must ask for appropriations. Stockpiles are a recent development, stemming from the 1946 Strategic and Critical

Materials Stockpiling Act.[44] An example of their usefulness to a President occurred in 1965 when Lyndon Johnson decided to change the American role in Vietnam by bombing in the North. He was able to expand American involvement into an actual war and sustain that involvement out of existing stockpiles at his command. It was not until the spring of 1966 that he had to turn to Congress for a specific war appropriation. By that time it was too late for Congress to have a part in the decision-making process. If it had failed to support the armed forces in Vietnam, general public response would have been "massive retaliation" against Congress. The President had framed the options in such an unattractive way that Congress had no real choice. He can always claim greater expertise to the public and get the backing of the Joint Chiefs. It is difficult for a commander to get a wide public hearing for his dissenting view since the Kennedy Administration instituted the requirement that all speeches be cleared with the White House prior to delivery. Moreover, the Joint Chiefs have many hostages to fortune in the President's ability to reorganize the military establishment and set force levels. An example of Presidential power along these lines was given after disagreement between the commanders and the civilian leaders on necessary force levels for Vietnam. The commanders had desired more than the President believed politically and economically feasible. To still rumors of disagreement President Johnson held a televised press conference which treated the American public to a series of Mandarin nods accompanying the following dialogue:

"The troops that General Westmoreland needs and requests, as we feel it necessary, will be supplied," Mr. Johnson said. "Is that not true, General Westmoreland?"

"Yes, Sir."

"General Wheeler?"

"Yes, Sir."

"Secretary McNamara?"

"Yes, Sir."[45]

This is not meant to indicate that the military services may not communicate their desires to Congress, *sub rosa*, but they are significantly limited in their capacity publicly to express dissent from their Commander-in-Chief.

Should Congress appropriate money for military items of which the President does not approve, he can impound the money, as was done in 1956 when Congress voted extra funds to expedite the building of bombers and tankers or in 1958 when Congress voted money to maintain the national guard at levels higher than those desired by the Executive. Because the President's position is so secure on defense policy, this is the major area where the Bureau of the Budget's impounding powers have been successful.

Even in the area of force levels and military public works, where Congress plays a much more active role, the Executive's power to say "no" is final.[46] Although prior to the Cold War Presidents often vied unsuccessfully with Congress for responsibility over weapons selection, since its advent, Congress has left this responsibility to the Executive.

Rather than functioning in the primary role envisioned by the Founding Fathers, Congress' role in defense policy has become that of lobbyist for particular programs and activities it wants to see encouraged, most of which are on the margins of military policy, not central to it. It lobbies through holding investigations (such as the national military posture hearings of the Armed Services Committees) and through attempts to pressure decision-makers by letters, speeches, phone calls, or giving information to journalists. Recent examples of Congressional success in lobbying for particular concerns have included Congress' prevention of a proposed merger of national guard and reserve units and protection of development plans for the RS-70 bomber, which President Kennedy had wished to terminate. Congress' primary influence recently has been in real estate transactions and public works projects of the military departments, for reasons of constituency politics.[47] It is this type of issue, marginal to the broad questions of military policy in terms of national or international goals, which is the principal focus of the House Armed Services Committee. One of the most experienced staff men on military matters on Capitol Hill was quoted as saying of that committee, "If you study our committee, you are studying real estate transactions."[48]

Congress is gravely handicapped in assessing the President's proposals on broad objectives in military policy because he has a monopoly of information in this sphere. Moreover, the general public gives Congress no guidance beyond a generalized desire for "a strong National Defense."[49] Whereas there is a highly vocal attentive public for questions of weapons development, military real estate transactions, military public works projects, and military reorganization, the specialized attentive public for broad questions of military strategy, goals and objectives is quite small.[50] As a result, the military exercises a near monopoly on presentation of alternatives to Congress. The widespread feeling of Congressmen has been found to be one of grudging acquiescence in military proposals, on the grounds expressed by one leading Representative on military affairs: "How the hell do we know that should be considered anyway. We mostly reflect what the military men tell us."[51]

Ostensibly, the military itself would be a check upon Presidential initiative in strategic programs, but it has generally been satisfied with the *status quo* and therefore passive with regard to making changes in strategy.[52] Because any major change in strategy involves overall change and adjustments in domestic and foreign policy, the military are in no position to innovate. Innovation must be the preserve of civilian administrative leaders. Thus, the President is in the fortunate position of being able to justify changes in his military policy to Congress on the grounds of advice from his military experts, whereas he can justify changes to the military on the grounds of his superior knowledge of the political realities of Congressional and public desires and the problem of allocating limited resources among domestic and military values.

Military policy, like foreign policy, is made in the innermost circle. Here there is a great deal of competition because of America's bureaucratic pluralism: civilian, military, and foreign service personnel are involved. Bargaining and compromise revolve particularly around the decisions of the Joint Chiefs of Staff and the National Security Council. Although the President may not personally formulate policies, at least his acquiescence is necessary for successful innovation. Therefore, here, as in foreign policy, he is the center of lobbying activity by various interests within the executive branch, but his is the controlling voice. Other people can raise the price of a Presidential decision (*e.g.*, the Pentagon may "leak" information to the press, or Congress may threaten retaliation against a key domestic program), but this is a control on the margins of power. If the President chooses to fight, his capacity to win in military policy is unusually high.

Presidential Liabilities

The limitations on the President include limitations of his own perceptions and political calculations and his capacity to attract able advisers. In questions of military policy, as in all other areas, the President may be limited by the capacity of the bureaucracy to absorb and deflect his initiatives. He is further limited by the politics of fiscal policy. Finally, it may be easier to become involved in the use of military force than to terminate such an involvement.

In many ways, the greatest limitation on the President in defense policy is similar to that in foreign policy—his ability to obtain good advice and use it intelligently. Military experts can be as myopic about their concern as can experts in any other field, but the President is responsible for selecting alternatives on the basis of a broad consideration of domestic and international goals. President Kennedy learned a bitter lesson through the Bay of Pigs fiasco in 1961 that "experts" should be heard with scepticism because of the narrowness of their interests. Therefore, he relied upon his own personal judgment to carry him through the Cuban Missile Crisis in 1962. On the Bay of Pigs he had deferred to experts against his better judgment—he managed the Missile Crisis himself.[53] Both Presidents Kennedy and Johnson were handicapped by the limitations of their two primary advisers on questions of defense, Secretary of State Dean Rusk and Secretary of Defense Robert McNamara. As has been mentioned, Dean Rusk proved to be a man incapable of innovative thought and therefore unable to present alternative strategies to those proposed by Robert McNamara. Into the vacuum left by an unimaginative Secretary of State, Robert McNamara rushed with superb self-confidence. He became the primary source of defense and foreign policies for both the Kennedy and Johnson administrations from 1961 to early 1968. In Kennedy's case the President had a background of wide and reflective reading in foreign and military affairs, coupled with experience on the Senate Foreign Relations Committee. President Johnson had less background in these matters and was correspondingly more dependent on Secretary McNamara.[54] Therefore, military criteria and military solutions received heavy attention. In the absence of a vocal Secretary of State, there was no voice for diplomatic or political responses that had the stature of the Secretary of Defense. Consequently, military solutions were the principal alternatives presented to the President.

Another factor limiting the President's capacity to innovate in military policy has been the politics of fiscal policy. Even the richest nation on earth does not have unlimited resources. Money spent on military programs will not be available for domestic ones, and *vice versa*. Therefore, the President is forced to solve two simultaneous equations: the ratio of American military force to that of other nations (especially the Soviet Union) and the relation between domestic and military spending. The second part of the equation has become increasingly difficult because of two factors: the pressures of growth in existing domestic programs coupled with new domestic commitments and a tendency toward erosion in the tax structure.

The modern service state is subject to a wide range of demands including highways, education, civil defense, medical research, Medicare, urban renewal, and poverty programs. New Deal and Fair Deal measures for agriculture, veterans, labor, and natural resources have continued to grow. Meanwhile there has been a tendency toward erosion of the tax structure, which has limited the growth of funds available to the government. The taxation level has tended to be frozen unless there has been a major political change from war to peace. Within that frozen structure a process of erosion has occurred through piecemeal tax reduction for those most politically powerful, followed by demands from other groups for equal protection. The combination of growing domestic spending with erosion of the revenue base results in a limitation upon the amount of money available for defense spending. Without a major increase in tax resources the administration must choose between "guns or butter." As has been discussed in Chapter II, the political difficulties in tax revision make this situation a serious limitation upon Presidential initiative.

A final liability that the President must face is the relative ease of military involvement as opposed to the difficulty of extricating the nation from such involvement. This has been amply demonstrated by the Vietnamese conflict. Any military involvement also concerns the nation's prestige. Fear of loss of prestige forces increased commitments. Such an expenditure of human and material resources is justified on the basis of American defense needs, and therefore supported by mass opinion. Yet the greater the expenditure of life and funds, the greater the public expectation of significant accomplishment. This provokes an escalation of military effort, and the vicious cycle continues as the pressures of domestic expectations and domestic critics limit the President's willingness to withdraw without "victory." In a limited war waged by guerrilla tactics on an extraordinarily difficult terrain, with only limited cooperation on the part of the South Vietnamese, the costs of the pursuit of "victory" can be incalculable.

Conclusion

The significance of the bargaining advantages inherent in the Presidential office are most apparent in the formulation of foreign and defense policies. As Chief of State, Commander-in-Chief, Chief Legislator, Chief of Party, Voice of the People, and Leader of the Free World, the President can be neither checked nor balanced by the Supreme Court or Congress, except on marginal issues. His prerogatives, the lack of Congressional organization for effective policy innovation in these areas, and the preeminent position he is accorded by public opinion, all contribute to an impression that Prometheus is indeed unbound.

The impression is fairly appropriate if constitutional bonds are considered, but there are other fetters on Presidential innovation in foreign and defense policy. The capacity of his bureaucracy to absorb and deflect his initiatives is one significant limitation. Another is posed by the politics of fiscal policy, still another by the difficulty of withdrawal from military involvement. A President's incapacity to attract able advisers or to stimulate debate from which he can gain information on policy alternatives would be a severe handicap. Perhaps the greatest limitation upon Presidential initiative in foreign policy and defense is a personal one—his judgment and sensitivity to the strengths and weaknesses of the advice he is given. Although the President is not the source of policy formulation, he must choose among the policies presented by his experts and advisers. As Richard Neustadt has suggested, "Nobody and nothing helps a President to see, save as he helps himself."[55] His position is unique in the American political system in terms of visibility, responsibility, and opportunity. Therefore, the President needs a sensitivity to the uses of power, and a sense of direction. Without the latter, the vast powers at his disposal cannot be effectively employed. Skill in using Presidential power is not judged without consideration of the purposes for which the power is being used.

V. Direction and Style

THE INEVITABILITY of change provides a stable element in the context within which a contemporary President must function. Whatever else may be altered over the next generation, the Presidency appears likely to remain the focus of accelerating demands and expectations as the nation undergoes turbulent technological, social, and economic revolution throughout the last third of the twentieth century. Thus, the office, which has already changed so much since the era of Franklin Roosevelt, will continue to be altered under the dual impact of routinization and institutionalization. Consequently, the paradox of the contemporary Presidency will deepen—its mixture of risk with asset, clerkship with leadership, exposure with isolation. The President will continue to be the prisoner of expectations and their routinization, of deadlines and events, and of a necessarily heavy dependence on the advice and alternatives presented by others, although he alone will be held constitutionally responsible for following such advice. A continued imbalance between the restrictions on his personal control in the domestic sphere, and his greater leeway in the sphere of defense and foreign relations also seems likely, although some restrictions may perhaps be added in the latter.

In order to cope with these pressures, any President will naturally require persuasive skill, political sensitivity, popular appeal, and a capacity to attract able men and use their ideas well. Yet his essential prerequisites will be none of these, but rather the intangible qualities expressed by the concepts of a "sense of direction" and "style."

A sense of direction encompasses many attributes, notably a recognition of the significance of the changes that are affecting his nation and a perception of the ways of preparing it to cope with such change. Thus, it includes the capacity for both reflective and creative thought. Such thought is founded on the development throughout his lifetime of a firm set of values, which provide the criteria on which to base his judgments. Perhaps this is another way of expressing the point made by V. O. Key that the crucial factors in determining the manner in which the political system will function are the values and goals of its elected leaders.[1]

As has been indicated, the President has become the primary source of initiative in the American political system. Domestic programs will lack direction if he does not supply it, (yet he will have to struggle to do so because there are many competing voices in the concentric rings in which domestic public policy is formed.[2]) His need for a sense of direction is even greater where international and military policy are concerned, because these decisions are generally made in the innermost circle, where his is the controlling voice, and he is *the* indispensable member of any innovating group. Within that innermost circle there is generally a wide variety of conflicting advice on every issue, all or none of which may be appropriate. The men who offer it, whether the Secretary of Defense, one of the Joint Chiefs, a member of the White House Staff, or the Secretary of State, each represent a different experience, position, involvement, and perspective than the President. The selection must be his.

Unfortunately high office is, quite literally, not foolproof. The problems posed by an inept leader are magnified by the fact that public opinion does not play the role expected of it by traditional democratic theory, especially in foreign and military policy. While amateurs in the Presidency must therefore be considered dangerous, skillful political manipulation is not sufficient either.

Naturally, no man lacking political skill could function effectively because he is involved in a decentralized, pluralistic political system in which decisions are made through a bargaining process. Concern for power is therefore necessary for any administration, but to be used creatively, that power must have consistent direction. Creative leadership, as opposed to skillful manipulation, requires that the President seek "not only to win votes but consciously to alter basic political forces such as public opinion, party power, interest group pressure, the governmental system."[3]

Direction shows in the pattern formed by an administration's decisions. No President can remake the country, nor "solve" the major problems facing it. He can only nudge it along the appropriate path. A series of undirected nudges is meaningless, like a man elbowing frantically in a milling crowd. Quantity of action is therefore in itself meaningless if not coordinated with a sense of direction—the effects of undirected actions may well contradict one another and cancel the quality of what is done. Quality is the stamp on the nation that an administration makes, enduring beyond the quantity of its acts. As one observer wrote, "Effective policy depends not only on the skill of individual moves, but even more importantly on their relationship to each other."[4] For example, President Kennedy's commitment to public school integration was undercut by his appointment of segregationists like Harold Cox as federal district judges in the South, at a time when these lower courts were needed to enforce the Supreme Court's integration decision.[5]

Because a President who fails to accomplish his goals during his administration may cast a shadow across the future, there may be worse things than "losing" for a President. The "art of the possible" is political wisdom to only a limited degree. Harry Truman understood this, and it was his great strength. In fighting many unsuccessful battles (such as those for civil rights and government financed medical aid for the elderly), President Truman helped to educate the American public, thereby laying a foundation that enabled his successors to accomplish his vision. A man with such a vision can attract others to government service. For example, Adlai Stevenson attracted to the Democratic party a group of imaginative, committed young men who helped to form the nucleus of support for John F. Kennedy. Dwight David Eisenhower attracted to Republican ranks a group of men who rejected the party's past isolationism. John F. Kennedy created a new sense of excitement and significance about government service which attracted many able people. Such contributions are highly significant because the policy choices that are made depend not on all the alternatives that are available, but on all the alternatives that are *presented*.

Therefore, the men who formulate the alternatives play a crucial role in governmental operations, and the President's sense of direction is the basis for both their recruitment and utilization of their alternatives.

A sense of direction is thus crucial for effective Presidential performance, but it must be reinforced by that illusive quality known as "style" to be most effective. Style includes a sense of proportion, a feeling for nuances, a capacity to interest, attract, and educate. A President's sense of direction will indicate what should be done, but his style will be the means through which he attracts and persuades others. For example, most biographers of President Roosevelt would probably agree with Arthur Schlesinger's assessment: "It was not any technical wizardry as a politician but rather his brilliant dramatization of politics as the medium for education and leadership which accounted for his success."[6] It was in this way that he and all those Presidents whom Americans consider great created a compelling national image.

American liberals judge their Presidents on the basis of their successful use of power to further the goal of creating a society within which the greatest possible degree of individual growth and development is possible. This is indeed a high standard, and one which few individuals can meet. The few who do possess the sense of direction and the style appropriate to their era are enshrined in the hearts of their people as great folk heroes. It is fortunate that at several crucial points in American history such individuals were available, yet tragic that they have not been nor will they always be at hand. There is risk as well as opportunity in this office upon which so much depends.

Notes

INTRODUCTION
[1] Louis Hartz, *The Liberal Tradition in America* (New York: Harcourt, Brace and World, Inc., 1955), p. 140.

[2] *Ibid.*, p. 50.

[3] Gunnar Myrdal, *An American Dilemma* (New York: Harper and Brothers, 1944), p. 7.

[4] Clinton Rossiter, *Conservatism in America* (New York: Random House, 1962), Ch. III.

[5] An excellent brief summary of the developments in liberal thought may be found in L. T. Hobhouse, *Liberalism* (New York: Oxford University Press, 1964).

[6] Edward S. Corwin, *The President: Office and Powers* (New York: New York University Press, 1957).

[7] Richard E. Neustadt, *Presidential Power* (New York: John Wiley and Sons, Inc., 1961).

[8] Clinton Rossiter, *The American Presidency* (New York: Harcourt, Brace and World, Inc., 1960).

[9] *New York Times,* Jan. 24, 1968, 38:5.

CHAPTER I
[1] "Supreme Court Requires Equally Populated Districts," *Congressional Quarterly Weekly Report,* XXII (Feb. 21, 1964), 352.

[2] Julius Turner, "Primary Elections as the Alternative to Party Competition in 'Safe' Districts," *The Journal of Politics,* XV (1953), pp. 197–210.

[3] *Ibid.*

[4] For a fuller discussion of the effect of seniority on Congressional relations with the President, see Chapter III.

[5] V. O. Key, *American State Politics* (New York: Alfred A. Knopf, 1956), pp. 145–152.

[6] Table 10-1, "Summary of the Distribution of 1956 Voters in Levels of Conceptualization," Angus Campbell, Phillip E. Converse, Warren

E. Miller, and Donald E. Stokes, *The American Voter* (New York: John Wiley and Sons, Inc., 1960), p. 249.

[7] V. O. Key, *The Responsible Electorate* (Cambridge, Mass.: The Belknap Press, 1966), Ch. IV.

[8] This argument is further developed by Judson L. James, *American Political Parties: Potential and Performance* (New York: Pegasus, 1969), Chapter 7.

[9] Donald R. Matthews and James W. Prothro, *Negroes and the New Southern Politics* (New York: Harcourt, Brace and World, Inc., 1966), pp. 383–384.

[10] Campbell *et al., op. cit.,* Ch. 3.

[11] Key, *American State Politics,* p. 33.

[12] See Theodore H. White, *The Making of the President 1960* (New York: Atheneum Publishers, 1961). Unless otherwise noted, all references to the 1960 campaign are based on this volume.

[13] Theodore H. White, *The Making of the President 1964* (New York: The New American Library, 1965). Unless otherwise noted, all references to the 1964 campaign are based on this volume.

[14] See Cabell Phillips, *The Truman Presidency* (New York: The Macmillan Co., 1966).

[15] To use the role designations of Clinton Rossiter, *The American Presidency.*

[16] Gerald Pomper, *Nominating the President* (New York: W. W. Norton and Co., 1966), pp. 61–63.

[17] Rowland Evans and Robert Novak, *Lyndon B. Johnson: The Exercise of Power* (New York: The New American Library, 1966), *passim.*

[18] Theodore C. Sorensen, *Kennedy* (New York: Harper and Row, 1966), p. 74.

[19] Richard Reeves, "Nixon's Men Are Smart But No Swingers," *New York Times Magazine* (Sept. 29, 1968), pp. 28–29, 127–132.

[20] Philip E. Converse, Aage R. Clauson, and Warren E. Miller, "Electoral Myth and Reality: The 1964 Election," *American Political Science Review,* LIX (June, 1965), pp. 321–336.

[21] Pomper, *op. cit.,* pp. 8–9.

[22] *Ibid., passim.*

[23] Nelson W. Polsby and Aaron B. Wildavsky, *Presidential Elections* (New York: Charles Scribner's Sons, 1968), pp. 122–123.

[24] H. A. Simon and Frederick Stern, "The Effect of Television Upon Voting Behavior in Iowa in the 1952 Presidential Election," *American Political Science Review,* XLIX (June, 1955), pp. 470–477.

[25] Lewis A. Froman, Jr., "A Realistic Approach to Campaign Strat-

egies and Tactics" in *The Electoral Process,* ed., M. Kent Jennings and L. Harmon Zeigler (Englewood Cliffs, N.J.: Prentice Hall, Inc., 1966), pp. 5–11.

[26] Stimson Bullitt, *To Be A Politician* (Garden City, New York: Doubleday and Co., 1961). For further discussion of the expense of the nominating process see Paul T. David, Ralph M. Goldman, and Richard C. Bain, *The Politics of National Party Conventions* (New York: Vintage Books, 1964), pp. 14–17, and Donald R. Matthews, *U.S. Senators and Their World* (Chapel Hill: University of North Carolina Press, 1960).

[27] Paul T. David, ed., *The Presidential Election and Transition 1960–1961* (Washington, D.C.: The Brookings Institution, 1961).

[28] Dean E. Mann, "The Selection of Federal Political Executives," *American Political Science Review,* LVIII (March, 1964), pp. 81–99.

CHAPTER II

[1] Campbell *et al., op. cit.,* p. 60.

[2] The following discussion of media use is based, unless otherwise cited, on Elmer E. Cornwell, Jr., *Presidential Leadership of Public Opinion* (Bloomington, Indiana: Indiana University Press, 1965).

[3] Sorensen, *op. cit.,* p. 356.

[4] Cornwell, *op. cit.,* p. 152.

[5] Fletcher Knebel, "The Campaign and the Candidates," 28 *Look* (Nov. 3, 1964), p. 24.

[6] Cornwell, *op. cit.,* p. 267.

[7] *Ibid.,* p. 272.

[8] *Ibid.,* p. 284.

[9] Sorensen, *op. cit.,* pp. 361–365.

[10] Cornwell, *op. cit.,* p. 4.

[11] *Ibid.,* p. 205.

[12] Sorensen, *op. cit.,* p. 368.

[13] *New York Times,* Jan. 12, 1966, 14:3.

[14] Cornwell, *op. cit.,* pp. 210–211.

[15] Roger S. Allen and William V. Shannon, *The Truman Merry-Go-Round* (New York: Vanguard, 1950), pp. 54–56.

[16] Cornwell, *op. cit.,* p. 218.

[17] *Ibid.,* p. 221.

[18] *Ibid.,* p. 294.

[19] *Ibid.,* p. 302.

[20] V. O. Key, *Public Opinion and American Democracy* (New York: Alfred A. Knopf, 1961), pp. 552–556.

[21] See Robert Conot, *Rivers of Blood, Years of Darkness* (New York:

Bantam, 1967), and *Report of the National Advisory Commission on Civil Disorders* (New York: Bantam, 1968).

[22] Grant McConnell, *Steel and the Presidency*, 1962 (New York: W. W. Norton and Co., Inc., 1963), p. 115.

[23] E. S. Flash, *Economic Advice and Presidential Leadership: The C. E. A.* (New York: Columbia University Press, 1965); Alvin Hansen, *The American Economy* (New York: McGraw-Hill, 1957), p. 87.

[24] Walter Heller, *New Dimensions of Political Economy* (New York: W. W. Norton and Co., 1967).

[25] McConnell, *op. cit.*, p. 84.

[26] Evans and Novak, *op. cit.*, pp. 419–420.

[27] Alex B. Lacy, Jr., "The Development of the White House Office, 1939–1967," unpublished paper prepared for delivery at the 1967 Annual Meeting of the American Political Science Association., p. 19.

[28] James W. Davis and Randall B. Ripley, "The Bureau of the Budget and Executive Branch Agencies: Notes on Their Interaction," *The Journal of Politics*, 29 (November, 1967), p. 752.

[29] Richard E. Neustadt, "Presidency and Legislation: The Growth of Central Clearance," *American Political Science Review*, XLVIII (Sept., 1954), pp. 641–671.

[30] Aaron Wildavsky, *The Politics of the Budgetary Process* (Boston: Little, Brown and Co., 1964), p. 40.

[31] *Ibid.*, p. 35 and pp. 35–42 *passim*.

[32] *Ibid.*, p. 41.

[33] Tom Wicker, *New York Times*, Jan. 30, 1968, 40:6.

[34] John F. Manley, "Wilbur D. Mills," unpublished paper prepared for delivery at the 1968 Annual Meeting of the American Political Science Association.

[35] Max Frankel, *New York Times*, Jan. 8, 1968, 52:2.

[36] Richard E. Neustadt, "Presidency and Legislation: Planning the President's Program," *American Political Science Review*, XLIV (December, 1955), pp. 980–1021.

[37] See Paul David, "The Vice Presidency: Its Institutional Evolution and Contemporary Status," *The Journal of Politics*, 29 (November, 1967), pp. 721–748.

[38] White, *1960*, p. 173.

[39] High executive support scores in marginal districts were found by Samuel C. Patterson, "Dimensions of Voting Behavior in a One-Party State Legislature," *Public Opinion Quarterly*, XXVI (Summer, 1962), pp. 185–201; and Lewis A. Froman, Jr., *Congressmen and Their Constituencies* (Chicago: Rand McNally, 1963), pp. 116–117.

[40] Arthur M. Schlesinger, Jr., *A Thousand Days* (Boston: Houghton Mifflin Co., 1965).

[41] An important critique of summit conferences was written before the 1960 election in *Foreign Affairs* by a foundation executive named Dean Rusk.

[42] No longer on the National Security Council.

[43] Roger Hilsman, *To Move a Nation: The Politics of Foreign Policy in the Administration of John F. Kennedy* (Garden City, New York: Doubleday and Co., Inc., 1967), p. 19.

[44] Lacy, *op. cit.*, pp. 24–25.

[45] Sorensen, *op. cit.*, p. 346, and Schlesinger, *op. cit.*, pp. 295–296.

[46] Sorensen, *op. cit.*, p. 319.

[47] *Ibid.*

[48] Schlesinger, *op. cit.*, p. 420.

[49] *Ibid.*, pp. 802–806.

[50] *Ibid.*, pp. 992–997.

[51] A Report by the Science Policy Research Division of the Legislative Reference Service, Library of Congress, for the Military Operations Subcommittee of the Committee on Government Operations (Washington: U.S. Government Printing Office, 1967), p. 2.

[52] Lacy, *op. cit.*, p. 15.

[53] *Ibid.*, p. 23.

[54] *Ibid.*

[55] Sherman Adams, *First Hand Report* (New York: Harper, 1961), p. 81.

[56] Evans and Novak, *op. cit.*, Ch. 9. See also Lacy, *op. cit.*, p. 26.

[57] Sir Alan P. Herbert quoted in Robert MacGregor Dawson, *The Government of Canada* (Toronto: University of Toronto Press, 1954), p. 235.

[58] Cornwell, *op. cit.*, p. 243.

[59] "How Much Management of the News?", *Newsweek*, 61:59–63 (Apr. 8, 1963), p. 60.

[60] For further discussion of this technique see Sorensen, *op. cit.*, pp. 288–297.

[61] Lacy, *op. cit.*, p. 31.

[62] Evans and Novak, *op. cit.*, *passim.*

[63] Cornwell, *op. cit.*, pp. 284–285.

[64] Corwin, *op. cit.*, p. 297.

[65] Theodore C. Sorensen, *Decision-Making in the White House* (New York: Columbia University Press, 1963), p. 83.

[66] *Ibid.*, Ch. 2 and 3.

[67] William Manchester, *The Death of a President* (New York:

Harper and Row, 1967), p. 481.

[68] Robert Donovan, *Eisenhower: The Inside Story* (New York: Harper and Bros., 1956).

[69] Mann, *op. cit.*, pp. 82–92.

CHAPTER III

[1] William S. White, *Citadel: The Story of the U.S. Senate* (New York: Harper and Bros., 1957), p. 12.

[2] This group struggle is the central focus of Bertram M. Gross, *The Legislative Struggle: A Study in Social Combat* (New York: McGraw-Hill, 1953).

[3] For fuller discussion of the development of standing committees see Leonard D. White, *The Federalists* (New York: The Macmillan Co., 1959).

[4] Raymond E. Wolfinger and Joan Heifetz, "Safe Seats, Seniority and Power in Congress," *American Political Science Review*, IX (June, 1965), pp. 337–349.

[5] "Judge" Smith's techniques are detailed in Nelson W. Polsby, *Congress and the Presidency* (Englewood Cliffs, N.J.: Prentice-Hall, Inc., 1964), pp. 72–76.

[6] Joseph P. Harris, *Congressional Control of Administration* (Garden City, N.Y.: Doubleday and Co., Inc., 1964).

[7] John Bibby and Roger Davidson, *On Capitol Hill* (New York: Holt, Rinehart and Winston, Inc., 1967), p. 17.

[8] Kennedy's dissatisfaction with his Secretary of State is discussed in Schlesinger, *A Thousand Days*, pp. 433–437.

[9] Bibby and Davidson, *op. cit.*, pp. 16–17.

[10] Fred I. Greenstein, *Children and Politics* (New Haven: Yale University Press, 1967), pp. 88–89.

[11] Roger H. Davidson, David M. Kovenock, and Michael K. O'Leary, *Congress in Crisis* (Belmont, California: Wadsworth Publishing Co., Inc., 1966), Ch. 2.

[12] *Ibid.*, p. 64.

[13] Polsby, *op. cit.*, pp. 107–108.

[14] Milton E. Cummings, Jr., *Congressmen and the Electorate* (New York: The Free Press, 1966), pp. 11–12.

[15] Patterson, *loc. cit.*, and Froman, *loc. cit.*

[16] H. Douglas Price, "The Electoral Arena," in David B. Truman, ed., *The Congress and America's Future* (Englewood Cliffs, N.J.: Prentice-Hall, Inc., 1965), p. 44.

[17] Lawrence H. Chamberlain, *The President, Congress and Legislation* (New York: Columbia University Press, 1946).

[18] Neustadt, "Planning the President's Program," *op. cit.*

[19] James Sundquist, *Politics and Policy* (Washington, D.C.: The Brookings Institution, 1968).

[20] Bibby and Davidson, *op. cit.*, p. 238.

[21] Evans and Novak, *op. cit.*, p. 498.

[22] David B. Truman, *The Congressional Party* (New York: John Wiley and Sons, Inc., 1959).

[23] For fuller discussion of the Congressional maneuvering see Bibby and Davidson, pp. 238–248.

[24] For the growth of the number of public employees from 1929 to 1962 see Frederick C. Mosher and Orville F. Poland, *The Costs of American Government* (New York: Dodd, Mead and Co., 1964), p. 141.

[25] C. Northcote Parkinson, *Parkinson's Law* (Boston: Houghton Mifflin Co., 1957).

[26] Stephen K. Bailey, *The New Congress* (New York: St. Martin's Press, 1966), p. 29.

[27] I am indebted to Wallace S. Sayre for this idea.

[28] Arthur A. Maass, "Congress and Water Resources" in Francis E. Rourke, ed., *Bureaucratic Power and National Politics* (Boston: Little, Brown and Co., 1965), pp. 101–114.

[29] David B. Truman, *The Governmental Process* (New York: Alfred A. Knopf, 1958), pp. 404–410.

[30] J. Leiper Freeman, *The Political Process* (New York: Random House, 1965) demonstrates the reciprocal nature of influence in committee-agency relations.

[31] The concept of a "cozy little triangle" is similar to the concept of "subgovernments" in Douglas Cater, *Power in Washington* (New York: Random House, 1964) or of "policy whirlpools" in Ernest S. Griffith, *Congress, Its Contemporary Role* (New York: New York University Press, 1961).

[32] Richard Fenno, *The President's Cabinet* (New York: Alfred A. Knopf, 1959).

[33] Glendon A. Schubert, Jr., *The Presidency in the Courts* (Minneapolis: University of Minnesota Press, 1957), p. 347.

[34] *United States v. Curtiss-Wright Export Corporation* (1936).

[35] *Youngstown Sheet and Tube Co. v. Sawyer* (1952).

[36] *Myers v. United States* (1926).

[37] *Humphrey's Executor v. United States* (1935).

[38] *Weiner v. United States* (1958).

[39] Samuel Krislov, *The Supreme Court in the Political Process* (New York: Macmillan, 1965), p. 140.

[40] Cornwell, *op. cit.*, p. 299.

CHAPTER IV

[1] *New York Times,* Nov. 22, 1967, 12:2.

[2] Campbell *et al., op. cit.,* pp. 182–183.

[3] *Ibid.,* p. 199.

[4] V. O. Key, Jr., *Public Opinion and American Democracy* (New York: Alfred A. Knopf, 1961), p. 213.

[5] William C. Rogers, Barbara Stuhlar, and Donald Koenig, "A Comparison of Informed and General Public Opinion on U.S. Foreign Policy," *Public Opinion Quarterly,* XXXI (Summer, 1967), pp. 242–252, 251.

[6] Gabriel A. Almond, *The American People and Foreign Policy* (New York: Frederick A. Praeger, 1961), p. 72.

[7] Key, *Public Opinion,* p. 256.

[8] Roberta A. Sigel, "Image of the American Presidency—Part II of an Exploration into Popular Views of Presidential Power," *Midwest Journal of Political Science,* X (Feb., 1966), pp. 123–137, 125.

[9] *Ibid.,* p. 126.

[10] This is the thesis of James A. Robinson, *Congress and Foreign Policy* (Homewood, Illinois: The Dorsey Press, 1967).

[11] *Ibid.,* p. 15.

[12] *Ibid.,* p. 177.

[13] Mark Kesselman, "Presidential Leadership in Congress on Foreign Policy: A Replication of a Hypothesis," *Midwest Journal of Politics,* IX (1965), pp. 401–406.

[14] Text of Resolution, *New York Times,* Aug. 19, 1967, 10:4.

[15] *New York Times,* Nov. 12, 1967, E4:4.

[16] Hilsman, *op. cit.,* Ch. 35.

[17] These judgments are based primarily upon reading in Hilsman, Schlesinger, and Sorensen.

[18] Richard H. Rovere, *Senator Joe McCarthy* (New York: The World Publishing Co., 1959), pp. 32–33.

[19] Schlesinger, *op. cit.,* p. 413.

[20] This discussion of the CIA relies upon a series of articles in the *New York Times* in April, 1966: April 25, 1:2; April 26, 30:6; April 27, 1:2; April 28, 1:2; and April 29, 1:4.

[21] This is a primary criticism of his Presidency posed by James MacGregor Burns, *Roosevelt: The Lion and the Fox* (New York: Harcourt, Brace and Co., 1956).

[22] Phillips, *op. cit.,* p. 287.

[23] Almond, *op. cit.,* pp. xiv, xv.

[24] Emmet John Hughes, *Ordeal of Power* (New York: Atheneum, 1963).

[25] George F. Kennan, *American Diplomacy 1900–1950* (New York: The New American Library, 1957), p. 91.

[26] Schlesinger, *A Thousand Days,* pp. 434–435.

[27] Hilsman, *op. cit.,* p. 43.

[28] Schlesinger, *A Thousand Days,* p. 551.

[29] Hilsman, *op. cit.,* p. 599.

[30] Evans and Novak, *op. cit.,* p. 391.

[31] Samuel P. Huntington, *The Common Defense* (New York: Columbia University Press, 1961), p. 126.

[32] Key, *op. cit.,* pp. 31, 32.

[33] Huntington, *op. cit.,* pp. 235–239.

[34] Sigel, *op. cit.,* p. 126.

[35] Huntington, *op. cit.,* pp. 250–251.

[36] *Ibid.,* p. 242.

[37] *Ibid.,* p. 128.

[38] Walter Millis, *Arms and Men* (New York: The New American Library, 1956), p. 283.

[39] Expressed in National Security Council 68.

[40] The superior tactical flexibility argument was developed in opposition to a widely accepted theory that early American defeats were the result of sheer weight of enemy numbers in T. R. Fehrenbach, *This Kind of War* (New York: The Macmillan Co., 1963), pp. 147–156.

[41] The events of the dismissal are briefly summarized in Neustadt, *op. cit.,* Ch. 2.

[42] *New York Times,* Aug. 18, 1967, 14:3.

[43] *New York Times,* March 13, 1968, 1:1.

[44] For a fuller discussion of the development and implications of strategic stockpiles see Glenn H. Snyder, *Stockpiling Strategic Materials* (San Francisco: Chandler Publishing Co., 1966).

[45] *New York Times,* July 14, 1967, 1:8.

[46] Huntington, *op. cit.,* p. 130.

[47] Raymond H. Dawson, "Innovation and Intervention in Defense Policy," in Robert L. Peabody and Nelson W. Polsby, eds., *New Perspectives on the House of Representatives* (Chicago: Rand McNally and Co., 1963), p. 283.

[48] Lewis Anthony Dexter, "Congressmen and the Making of Military Policy," in Peabody and Polsby, *op. cit.,* p. 312.

[49] *Ibid.,* p. 313.

[50] Bernard C. Cohen, "The Military Policy Public," *Public Opinion Quarterly,* XXX (Summer, 1966), pp. 200–211.

[51] Quoted in Dexter, *op. cit.,* p. 315.

[52] Huntington, *op. cit.*, p. 22.

[53] Both Hilsman and Schlesinger detail the two Cuban crises.

[54] Evans and Novak, *op. cit.*, Ch. 22–24.

[55] Neustadt, *op. cit.*, p. 151.

CHAPTER V

[1] Key, *Public Opinion*, p. 540.

[2] Roger Hilsman's concept of policy-making in concentric rings is discussed in Chapter IV.

[3] Burns, *op. cit.*, p. 402.

[4] Henry A. Kissinger, *The Necessity for Choice* (New York: Harper and Brothers, 1961), p. 345.

[5] See Chapter III for a fuller discussion of this point.

[6] Arthur M. Schlesinger, Jr., *The Coming of the New Deal* (Boston: Houghton Mifflin Co., 1958), p. 573.

Index